To my darling (A/K/A head of Nt'l History Dept ) from her great admirer, his mark ✳

# Handy to Home

# Handy to Home

## A Lifetime in the Maine Outdoors

*Essays and Art by*
**Tom Hennessey**

SILVER
QUILL PRESS

Camden / Maine

Text and cover design by Michael Steere
Cover paintings by Tom Hennessey
    Front: *Net Profit*
    Back: *Finders Keepers*

Printed in China by Oceanic Graphic Printing, Inc.


9    8    7    6    5    4    3    2    1


Silver Quill Press is an imprint of:
Down East Books
P.O. Box 679
Camden, ME 04843
BOOK ORDERS: 1-800-685-7962

Library of Congress Cataloging-in-Publication Data

Hennessey, Tom, 1937–
        Handy to home : a lifetime in the Maine outdoors / Tom Hennessey.
            p.  cm.
        ISBN 0-89272-493-5 (hc.)
        1. Hennessey, Tom, 1937– 2. Maine—In art. I. Title

NC975.5.H48 A35 2000
814'.54—dc21
                                                99-086885

For all those who prefer pine-needled trails to pavement

# Foreword

On my office wall, just three feet away as I write this, is an extraordinary watercolor, one of only two originals in my meager but cherished collection of waterfowl art.

It is a dawn scene in which hues of peach, rose, and gray are beginning to define the sky above a Maine duck marsh. In the distance, shrouded in the chill mist rising off the water, is the silhouette of a sculling boat being poled quietly toward some unseen point, chosen long before the season opened by the two hunters on board. Despite their efforts at stealth, however, the boat's passing has flushed a pair of black ducks from the channel in the foreground. They have sprung skyward as only blacks do, their white wing linings catching the early-morning light, their bright-orange legs standing out against the characteristic dark brown of their plumage.

I bought this painting a decade ago not just because it was superbly crafted but because I have lived that exact scene and felt its beauty and drama. Tom Hennessey painted it for precisely the same reason.

Self-taught, Tom writes, draws, and paints from experience—*his* experience in the Maine outdoors, where he has spent every spare hour of a lifetime. And if there's anybody who more simply and effectively captures the smells, sounds, shapes, and memories of hunting, fishing, camping, and canoeing in our extraordinary state, I haven't met him.

So, when I became an editor at Down East Books three years ago, I immediately set about persuading our publisher—and then Tom, himself—that it was high time we put together a book to showcase the wonderful range of images Tom Hennessey has created over the years with his typewriter, watercolor brushes, pens, and graphite pencils.

As the editor of *Handy to Home,* I've read and reread the essays within at least half a dozen times, and they still move and delight me. I continue to be astonished at this artist's uncanny ability to render a duck, salmon, or gun dog at just the right moment, so that each looks not posed but completely natural, sometimes in its awkwardness.

But of all the pleasures this project has afforded me, the greatest has been getting to know Tom Hennessey, a talented, creative spirit whose passion for the Maine outdoors is unparalleled. I'm intensely proud that I can now call him my friend.

Chris Cornell, Editor
Silver Quill Press

# Color Plates

# Handy to Home

## Handy to Home

Assuming you've signed hunting and fishing licenses, duck stamps, deer tags, and the like for forty years or more, it's safe to say you've logged more miles in pursuit of outdoor sport than Lewis and Clark covered on their historic outing. Chances are, though, a good many of those miles were traveled via "Shank's mare" or what was referred to in Uncle Sam's Army as the "Ankle Express."

Show me a Maine sportsman who remembers when deer were carried on the fenders of cars, when the cost of a cedar-and-canvas canoe was two hundred dollars, and I'll show you a man who probably recalls hunting and fishing out his back door, literally. If the tracks of such memories are fresh in your mind, surely you realize how much you took for granted. To point it perfectly, consider the adage: "You never miss the water until the well goes dry."

With that in mind, you have no doubt developed a powerful thirst for the days when, before going to work, you and a few hunting partners moved deer in patches of woods within walking distance of home. Nowadays, you often drive an hour or more to find a few acres that aren't posted. By the same token, you probably remember catching trout in a brook that was only a half-hour hike down the railroad tracks or potting partridges in the overgrown orchard behind the cemetery or jump shooting black ducks that pitched into the bog down back.

Great days, those were, and grand times. But as you well know, they are disappearing like stars in the dawn. While hunting mornings before school, never did I imagine that I would see times when a day's bird hunting included covers in three counties. That's still hard to believe, but my truck's odometer doesn't lie about the miles it registers to and from fishing and gunning grounds. The reasons, of course, are as obvious as crows on snow: increasing population and more posted land.

It isn't surprising then, that Mainers who seldom left their communities— let alone their counties—to flush a bird, stalk a deer, or hook a fish, nowadays travel great distances searching for sport. And I mean *great* distances. When today's younger anglers tell of fishing expeditions to Alaska, Montana, Labrador, and Argentina, those of us who remember not being able to sleep on the eve of our first trip to East Grand Lake are left with feelings of awe and envy.

You'd also be surprised at the number of Maine sportsmen who hunt elk in Wyoming, quail in Georgia, doves and ducks in Mexico, and geese in Texas or on Maryland's Eastern Shore. And more than a few hie off to Africa to set their sights on lions, leopards, and cape buffalo.

Tom Hennessey—

Having had the pleasure of toting rods and guns to sporting camps and lodges scattered across this country and a few others, I can understand the excitement attendant to planning such trips. And I'm sure that when you strike off to go, let's say, Atlantic salmon fishing in Russia or bird shooting in Scotland (where, by the way, sporting traditions still reign supreme), you can't help but wonder how you managed to get from here to there.

Granted, whether such trips are annual occurrences or once-in-a-lifetime experiences, they are adventures that become treasured memories. Forever, then, I will be grateful to the people who afforded me the opportunities to paint, from firsthand experience, sporting scenes involving legendary fishing and hunting grounds.

Yet, in all honesty, I have to say that in enjoying those privileges, I always felt something was missing. For example, in fishing, I didn't have to paddle or pole the canoe, or read the water to find a fish. Instead, a guide put me in the right place and told me which fly to tie on and where to cast it. While bird hunting, I didn't have to locate covers or handle the dogs, and when hunting waterfowl it wasn't my responsibility to figure winds or tides, or rig the decoys.

The gist of it was that, although I caught fish, I missed the essence of fishing. Likewise, I didn't have to hunt for the game I bagged; all I did was shoot it. And, frankly, that just didn't do it for me. What I missed was fishing and hunting out my back door, so to speak.

Naturally, a regimen is required at camps that accommodate a dozen or more clients. Otherwise, a potentially enjoyable hunting or fishing

trip would become a parody of Ginsberg's picnic. However, I admit to having trouble dealing with regimentation, particularly in regard to outdoor sport. It ruffles my feathers and rubs my fur the wrong way, if you know what I mean, and I'm sure you do if you take a far-flung hunting or fishing trip now and then.

With that in mind, and depending on how difficult it is for you to blow out the candles on your birthday cakes nowadays, I'm sure you realize how much the likes of you and I took for granted when we stepped out our back doors to strike off on hunting and fishing trips that didn't require us to leave town.

Great days, those were, and grand times.

# A Rowboat Remembered

## A Rowboat Remembered

In Kenneth Graham's magical children's book *The Wind in the Willows,* Mr. Toad, the self-proclaimed sage of the swamp, tells the muskrat there is nothing quite so exhilarating as messing about in boats. Judging from the traffic on the water nowadays, it's obvious that Mr. Toad's words were imprinted on more than a few young minds.

It's safe to say, though, that most of the people raised in this neck of the woods were introduced to boats through fishing. It came with the territory, as they say. If you remember outboards with self-contained gas tanks, you know fishing boats of that era didn't have windshields and cur-

tained canopies to shed rain or water breaking over their bows, not to mention providing shade. No siree. The only protection a fourteen-foot Old Town or White boat offered against the elements was rain gear, take it or leave it. Come to think of it, that's all a sleek Grand Laker provides nowadays. Tradition is a tyrant, thank God.

Obviously, thinking about old fishing boats is like thinking about old friends: the farther back the friendships reach, the sweeter the memories become. Accordingly, I own five boats today—two canoes, a double-ender rowboat, a Merrymeeting Bay sculling boat, and an all-purpose aluminum outboard model that my wife refers to as a "tin can." Although each of the boats is filled with memories from stem to stern, none can compare with my reminiscences of an old rowboat that I messed about in a long time ago.

Over Orrington way, the "red bridge," as it's known to the native stock thereabouts, spans the marshy outlet stream of Fields Pond. Because the bridge was within easy bicycle distance of my boyhood home in South Brewer, I often fished there for perch and pickerel. The water I could cover, however, was restricted to the distance I could cast with an old level-wind Ocean City reel whose "anti-backlash" marking didn't mean a thing. Longingly, I gazed at the winding, unwadeable stream with its sprawls of pickerel weed and spatterdock. Constantly, I fantasized about catching bigger fish along its course, all the way to the pond and Brewer Lake beyond.

So it was that I began casting long, thoughtful looks at a rowboat berthed to the right of the bridge, heading toward Brewer Lake. Obviously, the skiff belonged to a snug brown house sitting handy to the marsh. One day, after watching perch rise far down the stream, I mustered enough courage to knock on the door. When an older man answered, I asked him if I could rent the boat for fishing. "I don't see why not," he said. "I only use it to poke around in now and then."

When I asked him what it would cost me, he replied, "How about a couple of perch?" Right then and there, I realized that I'd been rewarded for all the prayers I'd offered up for the poor souls in purgatory.

Years later, I boarded swift, fully equipped saltwater "sportfishermen" to try my luck on marlin and sailfish off Florida, Mexico, and the west coast of Costa Rica. But I'll say without hesitation, those boats didn't offer the excitement I felt the first time I launched that leaky, sun-bleached rowboat on Fields Pond stream. Need I say that it took only a couple of pulls on the oars for that

broad-beamed, tar-seamed ten-footer to become "my" boat?

To fit it out, I fashioned an anchor by filling an old paint can with sand and pounding the lid down tight. A coil of clothesline that I didn't think my grandmother would miss became my anchor line, an old coffee can served as a bilge pump, and strips of tin were tacked onto the oars' deeply split blades.

In short order, the boat's paint-scabby interior was sequined with fish scales, rusted hooks of all sizes sprouted from the gunwales, and tarnished spinners lay snarled in "bird's nests" of leader. The curled remains of sun-baked earthworms resem-

Tom Hennessey —

9

bled broken pretzels, and the bloated carcasses of sunfish and yellow perch—used for strip baits—looked like specimens dissected in a science class. To this day, I can smell the satisfying stink of that old rowboat.

Come fall, though, the fish scales were replaced with duck feathers. On Saturday mornings, before going to work, my grandfather would drive me out to the bridge. With my gunning gear stowed toward the bow and my springer spaniel, Snooky, sitting in the stern sheets, I'd row down the stream to set papier-mâché decoys on a wide, open turn. Come to think of it, a couple of those decoys are anchored in my den today.

There was no need to build a blind; I just camouflaged the boat with marsh grass and cattails, and shoved it into the shallows. When the morning flights of teal, black ducks, and woodies petered out, I'd sit on the boat's bow deck and, using an oar for a paddle, sneak along the stream's serpentine course in the hopes of jump-shooting ducks. When noon arrived I'd pull ashore, share my lunch with the dog, and then go pheasant hunting in the cornfields and covers that then bordered the marsh. Handy to four o'clock, when the mill let out, I'd be waiting at the bridge when my grandfather arrived to pick me up.

Eventually, however, I bought a canoe off the late Carroll Soucie. Consequently, I never again launched the old rowboat. It bothers me now that I never knew the name of the man I rented it from; I only know he wouldn't take any payment other than a few perch or a duck now and then. Obviously, I haven't forgotten him or the great days he afforded me a long time ago. But as focused as I was on fishing and hunting, I couldn't imagine why he kept a boat just to poke around in. Unless, of course, he once upon a time read *The Wind in the Willows.*

# Touchstones

# Touchstones

Although they don't readily admit to it, most sportsmen are sentimentalists at heart. Otherwise, their tackle rooms, gun closets, trophy rooms, attics, basements, dens, and other such sanctums—wives irreverently refer to them as "trash heaps"—wouldn't be top-heavy with touchstones.

Some people excuse such hoarding by alluding to intrinsic value. But I make no excuses for what I call my "comfortable clutter," the value of which is known only to me. Needless to say, the dog collars that were the sole property of my find-and-fetch hunting partners won't be fought over during the reading of my will. Neither will the duck calls given to me by an old gunner who remembered using live decoys, or the pair of ancient oars whose split blades pulled on more water than any sculling team ever would.

Admittedly, when I want to know what's in the bank or the checking account, I have to ask my wife. But I keep an accurate record of the whistles, knives, pack baskets, fish and game mounts, rods, reels, guns, snowshoes, and the like now adorning my den in dust-gathering retirement. Likewise the framed photographs, each dated by the color of my hair, and the battered decoys of my youth. Treasured images they are, but they also serve as sobering reminders that nothing lasts forever.

Recently, my wealth of touchstones was increased substantially by the addition of my tackle bag, which, according to my spouse, was no longer fit to take anywhere. Because her disparagement confirmed what I refused to admit, I grudgingly retired the dingy, threadbare bag by hanging it in my den. Henceforth, its pockets and compartments will hold only memories of people, places, and times the likes of which I'll never see again.

Oddly enough, exceptional fishing experiences played minor roles in my tackle bag's attaining touchstone status. To the contrary, small adventures and unexpected occurrences—not all pleasant, unfortunately—were the major players.

While salmon fishing at Helens Falls on the George River in Arctic Quebec, my Inuit guide, Sandy Annanak, took me to a small torrent that roared between the ledged shore and a huge, sheer-faced rock anchored in the river. Pointing to the boulder, Sandy asked, "You jump?" Judging the distance to be about six feet or so, I answered, "Sure." Beyond the rock, of course, was a prime holding pool.

"Me first," said Sandy. "You throw rod and tackle bag to me, then you jump." Before tossing the bag, I closed and buckled it tightly so that nothing would fall out. But even so, I held my breath when I threw it. If it had fallen into that gorge it would have been gone for good. Come to think of it, Sandy or I probably wouldn't have fared any better.

On a salmon-fishing trip to New Brunswick's Tobique River, my guide's setting pole broke as he snubbed the canoe downriver through a long stretch of rocky rips. In the next instant we were in the river, rolling and tumbling and trying to stand upright in the current that kept knocking us down.

Eventually, we succeeded and got hold of the canoe, which, luckily, wedged among some rocks.

When it was turned upright, I was relieved to see my tackle bag trapped beneath the bow seat. The camera stowed in the bag was never any good afterward, but losing it was better than losing boxes of flies and an extra reel and spools.

During a trout-fishing trip to Argentina I became friends with two of the most knowledgeable and accommodating trout-fishing guides I have ever met: Bill McPhee and Walter Wood. While leading me from pool to pool, each of them had occasion to carry my tackle bag, and neither failed to joke about its weight: "A man could get a hernia lugging this." Or, "How much did the

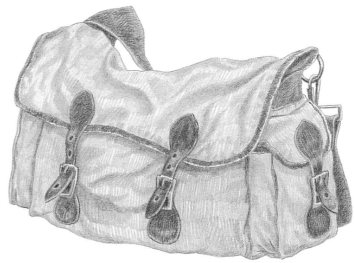

Tom Hennessey —

airline charge you for overweight baggage?" There were much more colorful remarks, too.

When the trip ended, we parted with plans to meet on Montana's Big Horn River. You can imagine my shock when shortly after returning from Argentina, I received word that Walter Wood had died from injuries suffered in an accident involving farm equipment. Then, only months afterward, Bill McPhee was killed in a plane crash. Only the good die young.

Obviously, I covered a lot of miles with that tackle bag slung on my shoulder. In addition to the aforementioned expeditions, the distances stretched to Alaska, Mexico, Costa Rica, the Bahamas, Montana, Florida, and, of course, fishing grounds scattered throughout Maine and Canada.

In fact, the sagging, fraying, and stained bag also accompanied me on hunting trips to Scotland, to Saskatchewan, and to southern quail and dove fields, where it carried rain gear, shells, binoculars, gloves, shooting glasses, gun oil, and the like.

But for my money, the most meaningful of all the memories contained in the now-retired tackle bag is the drizzly morning of May 1, 1986, when I caught the presidential salmon at the Bangor Salmon Pool. Making that memory all the more lasting is the fact that I caught this fish from a double-ended rowing boat, using a two-handed Thomas fly rod and a Hardy reel— all gear that was traditional at the once world-famous pool.

To me, that's reason enough for the old and tired tackle bag to join the displays of comfortable clutter in my den—my touchstones to people, places, and times the likes of which I'll never see again.

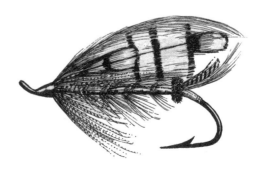

# Stripers and Streamers

## Stripers and Streamers

Sunlight spilling from a cloudless sky flooded the boat with warmth as I swung its bow into the tail of a long, foaming tide rip and eased the outboard down to trolling speed. Directly, the tip of my eight-and-a-half-foot fly rod trembled as a plastic Rapala minnow worked behind nine feet of leader and two colors of lead-core line.

If you've paid your angler's dues you know that, for the most part, fishermen reap benefits by being in the right place at the right time. No sooner had I spurred the outboard's ten horses into a quicker trot to compensate for the river's current when the rod did a back-bend that brought a round of applause from the reel.

Dead astern, the swirl blossoming on the sur-face signaled the beginning of a give-and-take tug-of-war that I won in less than five minutes but could have lost at any second. Held sculling alongside the boat, the striper measured eighteen inches on the tackle-box tape, typical of the "schoolies" that annually tend the tides in the lower stretches of the Penobscot River. When it was released, I watched the fish's silvery flanks become brassy as it disappeared into the river's dark-complected depths.

Now, if you've chased stripers, you've probably learned the meaning of the term, "fast fishing." Trouble is, the bass move with the tides, and the tides move constantly. With that in mind, I didn't waste any time jockeying the boat back into the tail of the rip, which was lengthening with the ebbing tide. For the uninitiated, it's not a good idea to troll directly through a rip or other area where stripers are stacked up. To do so usually puts them down, and that turns fast fishing into slow fishing in short order.

Trolling along the edge of the foaming flow, I was about in the same spot when the rod bucked and bowed again. That fish was the twin to the first one. Brace your feet: four more passes, four more stripers—ranging from sixteen to twenty inches, give or take. While one of the fish fought near the surface, three others chased it, obviously thinking it had found something worth eating.

Rowboat Remembered

Presidential Prize—Bangor Salmon Pool

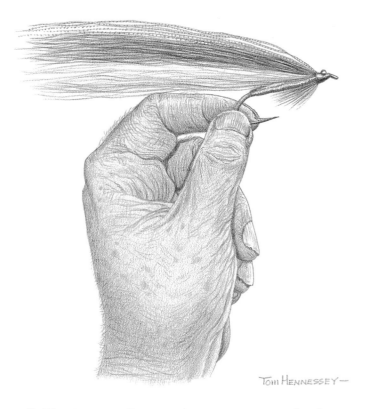

run tussle, the fish came unstuck and the Rapala floated to the surface where it worked slowly in the current. That's when a striper sucker-punched it. I didn't have to see it twice.

Quickly, I changed reel spools, replacing the lead-core line with a No. 6 floating fly line. After snugging a Joe's Smelt streamer (with a size 4X hook) to the leader, I positioned the boat about forty feet or so from the rip and cast into it. From then until the tide turned, those stripers hit that fly the way Sonny Liston hit Floyd Patterson. Talk about sport.

In all, Joe's Smelt accounted for fourteen fish caught and released, plus a couple of involuntary releases. If a legal-length striper—thirty-six inches at the time—was lurking in that rip, it was an antisocial fish. I'll admit, though, that while releasing one of about twenty-two inches, my mouth watered with thoughts of thick, white fillets fried golden brown and served with a salad.

At one point, while starting the outboard after the boat had drifted below the rip, I saw what appeared to be a seal off the starboard quarter. As my angle of vision changed, however, the object became two otters rolling and playing as they swam toward the opposite shore. Without a doubt, those agile anglers were also enjoying the fast action.

Suffice it to say, I was as happy as an otter in the Home Pool.

Remember the German boxer Max Schmelling's remark, "I see something," when he spotted a flaw in Joe Louis's defense? If you recall, Schmelling defeated Louis in a subsequent match. Well, while playing the next striper I hooked, I saw something. After a brief hit-and-

But there's more to fishing than catching fish. Soaring high in the clear, cerulean sky, an adult eagle's white head and tail feathers flashed like strobe lights. Golden sunlight silvered the wings of crows swooping from shadowy perches in towering pines, and an osprey hovered like a helicopter before folding its wings to plunge bomb-like toward a finned target. When the fish hawk struck the surface, it sounded as if a large rock had been thrown into the river.

It's no secret that fishing and contemplation are inseparable. While cruising back to the boat landing I thought about my friend Gene Hill, *Field and Stream* magazine's outstanding essayist. I had recently finished illustrating a book for Gene, who shortly thereafter lost his bout with throat cancer.

It would be difficult to find a man more appreciative of the aesthetic values of fishing and hunting than Gene Hill. No matter what we pursued—Atlantic salmon in Canada, trout in Montana or Argentina, birds and waterfowl in Scotland—he often paused to admire interesting landscape features or to ask sincerely, "Tom, what did you and I do to deserve being here?" Or, when the fishing wasn't up to snuff: "So what? If you were home you'd be working."

Needless to say, it would have been a bonus to have had Gene in the boat with me that day on the Penobscot River. It wouldn't have made any difference if the stripers had snubbed all our invitations. We'd have whiled away the time talking about rods and reels and guns and dogs, and surely he would have shown me an ungodly-looking salmon fly given to him by some Norwegian guide. Of course my response would have been something like, "Hell, even a pickerel wouldn't take that."

Without question, Gene would have said that the fast fishing I enjoyed that first day of summer was wasted on me. And allowing that I wasn't much more than a long cast from my house, I wouldn't have had much room to disagree with him.

A more beautiful day would have been unbearable.

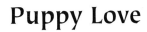

Puppy Love

# Puppy Love

Most men who train their own hunting dogs develop enough savvy to produce, say, an English setter that will point and hold birds, or a Labrador retriever that will find and fetch anything from a lost sock to a snow goose.

If you're a member of this august group, it's safe to say you're more than familiar with dog-training terms such as, "bumping," "blinking," "pottering," and "false pointing," all of which describe undesirable behavior and are commonly punctuated with, "You #@&*!" Of course you know annoyances of that ilk can be overcome by practicing patience and consistency. But let me ask you this: How successful have you been in overcoming the problem—perhaps I should say *problems*—of letting a pup coax its way onto your bed?

Can it be that all your vows, pledges, and promises never to let the youngster place so much as a paw on the bed were broken in the time it took to turn off the nightstand light? If so, you're probably a pushover for dogs, period. Young or old, mixed-breed or pedigreed, they're all special to you. That's all well and good. But if you're married to a woman who also is an absolute marshmallow when it comes to resisting a soft-muzzled, whimpering, tail-wagging "baby," mister, all I can say is you have my sympathy.

Seriously, if you've made the mistake of taking a puppy onto your bed, it's safe to say that you and your wife have learned to live with half the amount of sleep required for human beings.

Usually, it begins with the pup's yelping, crying, and clawing from inside the crate or cage that he's supposed to claim as his "territory." Shortly thereafter, it ends with your spouse's compassionate, "I'll let him sleep on my side until he gets used to his new home." So, with an I've-heard-that-before sigh, you roll over and fall asleep remembering the slogan once used in a whiskey advertisement: "Some thing's were never meant to change."

Now, tell me if I'm wrong: No sooner were you carried away by the arms of Morpheus when your dreams were shattered by, "Wake up! Quick, he has to go out! Get him . . . Oh, God, get some paper towels and the spray cleaner under the sink—not in the bathroom, in the kitchen! How long have you lived here? Never mind. You take him out. I'll do this. It's a good thing you weren't a mother."

I may be wrong, but I'm willing to bet that while you're stumbling around in the backyard mumbling "good boy" every time the pup squats, you now and then glance up at the stars and wonder if it's all worthwhile. Especially if it's midwinter, the temperature's below zero, and you're knee-deep in snow.

Speaking from experience, I won't hesitate to say you've been rousted from subliminal sleep more than once by the sounds of puppy teeth inscribing bedboards and by the rhythmical, pumping regurgitations that precede his upchucking God-only-knows-what. For the uninitiated, when any of the aforementioned occurrences jolt you into groping consciousness, never step out of the bed without benefit of a light.

If you've had the pleasure of being owned by a few puppies, you know their collar sizes change quickly. Accordingly, the pup that used to sleep comfortably on her side of the bed soon became a full-grown dog that sprawled wherever it wanted. I'm sure you'll agree it's amazing how a dog that can curl up on a handkerchief can uncurl to take up the entire foot of the bed, which, of course, leaves you and yours curled like pretzels.

Roll the dog off? Friend, you'd have better

luck trying to budge the Rock of Gibraltar. The most you'll get is an indignant groan and a dirty look. More often than not, it comes down to a matter of being damned if you do and damned if you don't. If you manage to move the dog and get him lying lengthwise on the bed, his sack-of-grain weight pulls the blankets down, leaving two night-chilled, unhappy campers.

Thank God for summer. During that season of heat and humidity, your prayers are answered as the dog seeks the cooler air that has settled near the floor. Once again you can sprawl and sleep comfortably. Want to bet? When the dog that has claimed your boudoir as his nocturnal re-treat wants out, he'll sit by the bed and grunt or whine his requests.

That's if you're lucky. If you're not, you may be awakened by a whack from a paw that leaves welts on your hide. Worse yet, some dogs think it's great sport to leap onto the bed and stomp and stumble all over you.

Naturally, the "little guy" you brought home becomes a "big guy" almost overnight. In fact, by the time you celebrate his first birthday, he has assumed the responsibility of defending his property and has developed a bark that would intimidate Beowulf.

Now that's just fine during the day. But in the wee hours, when his bellowed warnings sit you straight up in bed with your hair standing on end, it takes a few heart-stopped seconds to real-ize you're not about to be run over by a trailer truck or a train.

Believe me, sport, I know the feeling. And I fully understand that, if you do manage to get back to sleep that night or any other such nights, you'll drift into dreamland cursing dogs in gen-eral and vowing never to let another pup set foot in your bedroom—let alone put another paw on your bed.

# Planning Ahead

## Planning Ahead

Back along, a friend told me about a stream that meanders through miles of sprawling bogs and woodlands. "Lots of ducks in there," he said. "Woodies, mostly, but some teal and black ducks, too. It'd be a good chance to jump shoot, and it's a big enough area so you wouldn't drive everything out with one shot."

A blustery northwest wind buffed golden sunlight to silvery brilliance as I slid my fourteen-foot canoe into the stream a week or so later. The midmorning air was clear and cool, and not a wisp of cloud wrinkled the faded-blue canopy of sky. Stroking a paddleful of water astern, I allowed, "The Lord would never forgive me for wasting a day like this doing yard work. There's no doubt in my mind that today was created expressly for exploring new hunting territory."

Admittedly, hunting season is usually underway when I strike off in search of back-of-beyond gunning grounds that I was told were either "full of birds" or "alive with ducks." And usually I discover that the bird covers are too close to a house or a school and that the bog is no bigger than the Bangor municipal swimming pool. But not this year. No siree. This year I was going to do my homework so there'd be no chance of flunking out come opening day.

For once, it became obvious that my friend knew what he was talking about. Although the stream was a tad wide in places, its serpentine course provided cover enough for a canoe sculled with a silent paddle. That was proven when I eased around a point of willows rimmed with pickerel weed.

On the opposite side of the brush—I'd say less than twenty feet from me—a great blue heron spread its enormous wings and labored into the air as though in slow motion. The stork-like bird then scaled away with its long legs dangling and glided out of sight around the next bend.

I'd say that heron got as tired of looking at me as I did at it. During the course of my outing,

Tom Hennessey—

I must have disturbed it a dozen times. Each encounter, however, allowed me to admire the bird's camouflage and attendant instincts. Several times it remained statue-still as I approached, the curve of its head and long neck looking exactly like a twisted, weather-beaten snag.

True to my friend's prediction, the stream held mostly wood ducks. The first to take wing was a pair that boiled into the air as I hauled the canoe over a beaver dam. Not yet displaying their distinctive markings and plumages, the woodies immediately identified themselves with their shrill, tremoring cries. It couldn't have been a more appropriate location. On either side of the stream, the dark green crowns of oaks towered above the wind-tossed leaves of swamp maples.

Along that slow, winding, stump-strewn waterway, the surface of which was often stiff with spatterdock and other aquatic plants, I also flushed two larger flocks of wood ducks and a squadron of swift blue-winged teal. Come hunting season, it would, indeed, be a good chance to jump shoot.

Thoughts of hunting, however, went begging as I rested the paddle and studied a palette of colors that would clash on any canvas other than Mother Nature's. Framed by the rock-foundation remains of what was once a bridge, both banks of the stream were aflame with fireweed. Here, the florid magenta plants spread through the sun-splashed glow of green ferns and red cardinal flowers. There, they crept into clearings garishly cluttered with yellow goldenrod, white Queen Anne's lace, and purple joe-pye weed. How those colors all combined to produce such aesthetic appeal is far beyond me.

Not surprisingly, the bog teemed with wildlife. Red-winged blackbirds spilled liquid notes among swatches of cattails, and feeding kingfishers plunged from streamside perches. On a muddied hummock, the opened shells of fresh-water clams showed where a muskrat had enjoyed a midnight snack, and baritone bullfrogs sounded booming notes deeper than the mossy bottom of the stream.

But the show was stolen that day by painted turtles. Surely, I would be accused of exaggerating if I ventured a guess as to how many I saw basking in the sun. Practically every log was occupied by one or more of the colorful reptiles.

Wouldn't you know the wind swung around to buffet the small canoe head-on as I paddled back to my truck. With each stroke I cursed myself for not bringing my seventeen-footer, which would have tracked better and paddled more easily. But I suffered through it knowing

that when I headed for the stream come gunning time, I wouldn't have to drive around in the dark wondering which road and trail to take. Also, I'd know precisely the route of least resistance in sliding the canoe over the wooded bank to the stream.

Without question, preseason planning and exploring are important preludes to hunting season. Accordingly, as soon as I returned from the bog I remembered I had decoys that needed painting, dogs that needed running, boots that needed patching, outboards that needed tuning, and trailer lights that needed tinkering. And considering that there were only a few weeks to get everything done, I knew once again that the Lord would never forgive me for wasting a day on yard work.

# Whistlers in the Wind

# Whistlers in the Wind

Jeff, my oldest offspring, had tucked away two helpings at the hunters' breakfast and was contemplating a third when I said, "Forget it, we're running late now." About forty-five minutes later, the dawn breeze was blowing out the stars as the bow of our canoe crunched through shell ice rimming a grass mound in the upper Penobscot River.

"Grab those whistler decoys and set them along the edge of this eddy," I instructed as Jeff's Lab retriever, Magnum, lunged from the canoe. "I'll rig the blacks in this little cut. It's shallow all along here, but watch it you don't stumble over a rock and end up in the river; it's not exactly balmy this morning."

Directly, the breeze and the back eddies resulting from the river's current breaking around the grass mound added deceptive animation to the decoys. Swiftly we hid the canoe in the high, frost-fuzzy grass, and as we set up the portable blind of camouflage cloth attached to wooden stakes, the distant, rumbling of shotguns reached us.

"Good," I mumbled while stuffing No. 4s into my twelve-gauge pump. "A few hunters on the river will keep things stirred up." No sooner had I spoken when the clear, twittering wingbeats that are the calling card of the whistler, or goldeneye, spilled from a cloudless sky.

Ever notice that you seldom hear whistlers coming toward you? Usually, you don't notice their vibrant, chiming notes until the ducks are above, opposite, or going away from you, and it seems the higher they fly, the more clearly they're heard.

"Behind us!" Jeff warned. Against a grove of pines shading the Passadumkeag shore, white wing patches flashed like strobe lights as a single headed upriver. The duck didn't have enough altitude to see our decoys. But when it flew beyond the grass mound, it glimpsed our phony flock and abruptly banked into a toe-warming 180-degree turn. The only tighter maneuver I've ever seen was performed by my wife when, while driving, she spotted a yard sale on the opposite side of the road.

"All yours, Jeff," I allowed as the hen whistler came into range. Moments later, shell ice flew like shards of broken glass as Magnum charged into the water to fetch the bird, now floating feet up.

Ducks—a few blacks, mostly whistlers—trafficked steadily. Some saluted us by dipping a

wing toward the decoys as they passed, others cocked their wings and pitched down to scale by out of range, still others never gave us a second look. But there, friend, you have the essence of duck hunting—excuse me, of all hunting. Uncertainty is what kicks us out of bed at 4 A.M. to lug, drag, wait, watch, shiver, and—most of the time—wonder why things aren't working. If shooting a limit were a sure thing, hunting would be as boring as watching *Murphy Brown* reruns.

"Here we go," said my hunting partner with a nod upriver. "Two whistlers, way up." It appeared the pair were antisocial when suddenly they rocked, spilled air from their wings, and corkscrewed down to the decoys. One folded as our shotguns roared; the other didn't.

No sooner had Magnum fetched the duck than I saw a small flock approaching. Bigger birds, they were; with an undulating flight pattern uncharacteristic of whistlers. "Watch it, Jeff! Blacks coming down." Seconds later,

31

Magnum delivered my daily limit of one black duck. Behind me, Jeff was cursing his twelve-gauge autoloader, which hadn't ejected the first shell he fired.

If you've set your share of decoys, you know that no matter how intently you scan the sky, ducks will surprise you. I had just poured a cup of coffee when a winged shadow flew through the blind. The black had scaled in from behind and was only about twenty-five yards up. Unfortunately for Jeff, it was beyond us and out of range by the time we saw it.

By late morning, a brisk, biting northwest wind was trying to flatten the blind. There was no doubt in my mind that if we sat it out we could have filled our limits of three ducks apiece. It was only a matter of time. But when you've watched an eagle soaring and seen the wakes of bass feeding and heard the music of whistlers echoing in the November sky, a limit amounts to nothing more than a few more ducks to clean.

As always, while we were taking up the decoys, a pair of blacks came in below the tree line, lifted at the last second, and flew directly over us. Were they in range? We could see their eyes. Suffice it to say, Jeff's verbal barrage caused Magnum to walk away with his tail tucked between his legs.

"Not bad," I thought as we left the grass mound and paddled past an island where gray leafless oaks stood like gaunt old men. "Not bad at all. I've traveled a lot farther and paid a lot more to get a lot less."

# The Mad Miler

## The Mad Miler

You know how it is when you latch onto a promising bird-dog pup. You can't wait to turn the youngster loose in a cover. Admittedly, planted birds are great for starting a pup, but the sooner he encounters the paralyzing scent of wild birds, the quicker he will become a hunting dog.

So it was that I took my seven-month-old English pointer, Pete, into a sprawl of alders that were reclaiming a field at the foot of Whiting's Hill in Brewer. Although the breezy air felt cool, it was actually a bit humid. Therefore, my intention was to give the pup and myself a short workout.

After parking my truck, Pete and I cut through a swale that brought us to what traditionally were referred to as the "Bar Harbor tracks." We then followed the abandoned, alder-cluttered railroad bed under the overpass of Route 1-A. Beyond Burr Brook, we entered a field to the left of the tracks and started toward a stand of alders.

In the thick cover, Pete worked close, checking on me frequently. Pleased with his performance, I allowed that he really didn't need the dog bell rhythmically tolling his whereabouts—but I sure was looking forward to hearing it abruptly stop and silently shout, "Bird!" Directly, however, I noticed several unmistakable depressions in the goldenrods and hardhack bushes edging the alders—deer beds.

For obvious reasons, it's best not to work young dogs where there is an abundance of deer or other distracting game. The instinct to chase is strong in all dogs, particularly pups. Even while thinking, "I'd better take him out of here," I heard a deer jump—and heard Pete departing in the same direction. Charging after him I blasted on the whistle and yelled, "No, Pete!" "Whoa, Pete!" "Back, Pete!" and several other commands beginning with, "You" and ending with "Pete!"

If I could have caught the pup, reprimanded him, and left the area, it would have been a good

In Back of Beyond

Your Bird!

lesson. That, however, wasn't the case. The last I saw of Pete was when he crossed the tracks about fifty yards away and disappeared into the woods. For half an hour or so I walked, whistled, yelled, and listened to no avail.

Tom Hennessey

But because that neck of the woods was my hunting grounds as a teenager, the Bar Harbor tracks and the intersecting roads and power lines were trails I knew well. I was sure Pete would work back to the railroad bed, but I wasn't sure which direction he'd take then. My decision was to go back to my truck and drive to where the tracks crossed the Green Point Road, a mile or so away. From there I would follow the rails back toward Whiting's Hill, hoping to intercept Pete along the way.

When I began jogging, I quickly realized Pete wouldn't chase any great distance because of the humid heat. Awash with sweat, I stopped every hundred yards or so to whistle and listen. Nothing. At two power-line crossings I studied dirt paths and saw no dog tracks. Good. Eventually, after rounding a bend, I could see straightaway to the overpass at Whiting's Hill and beyond, a strong mile or more. And at that distance—to my great relief—I saw a white speck appearing and disappearing in the alders reclaiming the railroad bed.

At first I figured the young pointer had worked back to the tracks, cut my trail, and started backtracking. But, I thought, what if he wasn't backtracking? What if he just started running in that direction? Realizing that Pete could be headed for Holden, I started running.

Now, the next time I hear someone bragging about what great shape he's in because he runs a paved mile or so every day, I'm going to suggest he try racing a dog on a railroad bed of crushed rock while bobbing and weaving through alders to boot. With each crumbling stride, I cursed bird dogs, bird hunting, the "lightweight" label on my boots, the sound-smothering wind, woodcock, alders, railroad tracks and ties, humidity, and—most of all—deer.

I ran until I couldn't. Nearly exhausted, I stopped at Burr Brook and listened to my heart doing a drumroll in my chest. My legs ached, my feet hurt, my mouth and throat wouldn't have burned more if I'd swallowed burdocks. But while dousing myself with a hatful of water, I heard the distant tinkling of Pete's bell, and I responded with a short-of-breath blast on the whistle.

Shortly thereafter, I snapped the lead onto his collar and sprawled on the grassy bank bordering the tracks. "Pete," I said between licks at my face, "didn't your mother tell you about deer?"

Needless to say, the walk back to the Green Point Road and my truck was done at a leisurely pace. With Pete curled on the seat beside me— his puppy energy obviously drained—I pulled onto the road and stopped where the tracks crossed. Perhaps it was the humidity or the

overexertion or both, but as I stared along the overgrown railroad bed, the woods turned wintry and I saw a kid running between the tracks. He was toting a single-shot, sixteen-gauge shotgun and every now and then he stopped and listened for a pair of hounds that he last heard heading toward Whiting's Hill.

Laughing out loud, I headed home.

Seasoned with Wood Smoke

## Seasoned with Wood Smoke

One of the items deposited in my pack basket during the spring ritual of replacing hunting gear with fishing paraphernalia was a long-handled frying pan. Aside from the anticipation of filleted bass frying over an open fire, the sight of that stained and pitted skillet fanned the embers of old memories into flames.

Immediately, my den filled with the smell of wood smoke and the sound of a fire crackling on a graveled shore. I had about seventeen summers behind me then and figured it was high time I tried my hand at cooking something other than a hot dog over a fire. After all, if I became a guide or a game warden as planned, there'd be times when I'd spend days out in the williwags without the culinary pleasures of hearth and home.

No doubt you can recall a similar scenario. In fact, I'd say it was a good bet that you, too, had a poor excuse for a canoe stashed on the shore of, let's say, a marsh stream within walking distance of home. And unless I'm mistaken, you had a hunting and fishing partner who'd skip school on opening day, didn't pay much mind to mosquitoes or black flies, and figured that being cold and wet was better than being home.

Needless to say, neither of you were bashful about biting off more than you could chew. Small wonder, then, that you scoffed when experienced outdoorsmen told you that rustling up a meal in Mother Nature's kitchen was no easy task. "Hell," you replied, "if a man can't get himself something to eat he deserves to go hungry."

So it was that you and your partner set out to practice what you preached. The rucksack you toted to your canoe bulged and rattled with hatchet, frying pan, tin plates and cups, utensils, a billy for boiling tea, a can of Spam, several potatoes, two cucumbers, tea bags, a stick of butter, and a shaker containing mixed salt and pepper.

Directly, the canoe rocked gently as it was paddled swiftly—you always tried to outstroke each other—along the sprawling outlet stream

Tom Hennessey —

the fireplace would hold the billy while boiling tea. The Native American word for that arrangement was *chiploquorgan*. With that knowledge, how could you go wrong?

Shortly afterward, with the frying pan and billy in place, you struck a match and touched off the curls of birch bark and twigs beneath the pile of wood—all softwood, of course. Well, sir, speaking from experience, I'd be willing to bet that in jig time you had a fire going that Red Adair couldn't get near. Standing well back from the inferno, you and your partner allowed there'd be a great bed of coals for cooking when things simmered down.

In the meantime, you keyed open the can of Spam, peeled and sliced the potatoes and cucumbers, and broke out the butter and tea bags. The potatoes, naturally, would take the longest to cook so they'd be first on the fire. When the

leading to a pond. In a wind-sheltered cove you went ashore and wasted no time gathering kindling and wood while your partner arranged rocks to contain the fire. Next, you fashioned a grill by cutting and crosshatching green alder branches across the fireplace. A stout stick of alder propped with rocks so that it extended over

flames receded, you slid the stick of butter into the pan, which, of course, was so hot you couldn't touch it. Accompanied by a spattering sizzle, the butter disappeared as brown smoke billowed into the air.

Startled, your partner jumped sideways, his foot striking the alder stick and spilling about half the water into the fire. Now a cloud of white smoke and wood ash swirled upward. No harm done, though, you only needed about half that water, and a dash of wood ash was an appropriate seasoning.

Would you ever have believed it could take so long to fry potatoes? Each time you tested them with your knife they resisted, and when you finally removed them from the fire they were as brown and brittle as gingersnap cookies.

But it didn't take long to singe that Spam up in good shape. In about two minutes it was as curled and black as burnt bacon—which was OK because it smelled every bit as good. The tea? By then it had brewed to about the color of burgundy. What the heck, nobody's perfect and, besides, the cucumbers couldn't have been more delicious.

It goes without saying that anything cooked outdoors tastes better, and as you and your partner learned early on, the world turned slowly when you sat by a fire—well, after it burned down, anyway. Also, what better dinner music could you ask for than the laughter of loons or, perhaps, the booming notes of a bittern sounding like a pump that has lost its prime?

Unfortunately, what you think will last forever is soon gone forever. God only knows whatever became of the old canoe, your hunting and fishing partner is probably somewhere on the other side of the world, and nowadays "cookfires" are produced with portable gas stoves.

Admittedly, such fires are quicker, cleaner, and more easily controlled. Trouble is, though, there's no wood smoke to smell and no embers glowing with old memories.

# A Fish-Taker for Sure

## A Fish-Taker for Sure

No matter how many flies a person ties during the winter months, it's a sure bet that he or she will finish up by creating a special pattern designed expressly for the opening of the fishing season. It's just something that fly tiers do as part of the spring ritual, sort of like a woman buying a new Easter outfit each April.

With that in mind, let's fashion a streamer, a bright, clean, swift-looking fly to race like a spooked smelt on the landlocked salmon grounds. Let's make it a traditional tandem streamer, and let's make it long—say, about four inches, anyway.

After wrapping the connecting length of wire or leader to the fore and aft hooks, and lacquering the wraps in good shape, we'll secure the trailing hook—upturned if you prefer—in the vise and proceed to build a body.

Let's see now, what color? Orange? Nah, the Gray Ghost has an orange body. This fly has to be original. Silver? Uh-uh, there are too many streamers with silver bodies. I have to admit, though, they're all fish-takers.

What we want is something light with just a touch of color, something compatible with the flashing iridescent coloration of a smelt's flanks. Ah ha, there it is: pink, light pink floss. We'll rib it with silver tinsel—the narrower the better— just enough to catch the sunlight, if we should be so lucky, and reflect it with a flash. Better figure on two layers of floss to keep the color honest.

To start off, we'll wrap the thread—black monocord, actually—along the shank of the hook to where it begins to bend. Then we'll tie in the tinsel (don't forget to taper it!), and wrap the thread back to the eye.

Now we'll anchor the floss and wrap it smoothly down the shank to the tinsel, then smoothly back to the eye. There, we'll bind it down in good shape and clip it off. Now we'll form the ribbing with four evenly spaced turns of the tinsel. When we tie off the shiny stuff and

Tom Hennessey —

trim it, we'll leave just enough to bend backward and bind down. That'll prevent the resistance of the water from working the tinsel loose while we're trolling.

A tapered, whip-finished, lacquered head completes the trailing hook. Dress the lead hook accordingly, and we're ready to start fussing with feathers.

First, let's lay in several strands—keep it sparse—of iridescent Crystal Flash, long enough to extend beyond the trailing hook. Then we'll match up in length a barred Plymouth Rock hackle and two hackles of lead-gray—you know, that dark, bluish gray you see in a windy sky on East Grand Lake. Next, we'll sandwich the barred hackle between the gray hackles, position them atop the Crystal Flash, and bind them in place with a few turns of the bobbin.

What we need now is something to imitate the dark olive green of a smelt's back. To keep the fly slim and trim, how about four strands of peacock herl? That should do it. OK, now tie in a couple of jungle-cock eyes or cheeks, which-ever you prefer. (I call them eyes because that's what they look like.) Keep them fairly small and locate them near the head of the fly, not halfway back.

Now, turn the streamer over, and tie in a few strands of white bucktail that are as long as the hackles. To finish off the fly and at the same time add the extra touch that often makes the difference, clip a few fibers from a red hackle. Make them, say, about a quarter-inch long and tie them atop the strands of bucktail to represent gills.

Return the fly to the upright position, whip-finish the head, and apply a couple of coats of clear glossy lacquer. When the head of the fly is dry, wet your thumb and index finger and stroke the feathers, herl, bucktail, and Crystal Flash into a thin profile that should look swift and smelty even while anchored in the vise.

There you have it, sport, heave 'er overboard and drag 'er in near the rocks and brace your feet.

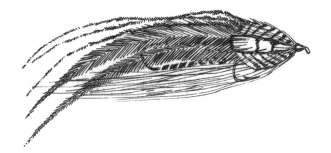

# The Thinker

## The Thinker

At this stage of the game I'm convinced that serious thinking requires serious sitting. In accordance with that, I suggest three places ideally suited for making monumental decisions: duck blinds, deer stands, and back steps. Obviously, the amount of intellectual exercise practiced in blinds and on stands is constrained by hunting seasons. Fortunately, there's no closed season on back steps.

Fact of the matter is, there's no better place for sorting out thoughts, especially if the steps are handy to a lawn that needs raking and rolling. That was the situation recently, when after fetching my outboard from the rafter-high clutter of the garage, I ambled toward the back steps. There, I sat and slumped into the elbows-on-knees, head-down position that seems universally accepted as most conducive to mind searching.

The morning sparkled with sunlight, and a brisk northwest wind buffed the sky to sapphire brilliance. The breeze, however, couldn't penetrate the high cedar hedge surrounding the backyard. The back steps, therefore, were toasty warm. Because my wife, an antiques dealer, was out making an offer on some great-grandmother's rolling pin or the like, I seized the opportunity to check my list of mental notes attendant to spring fishing. You understand, I'm sure, that solitude is necessary for such profound deliberation.

While robins played hopscotch on patches of bare ground, I studied the outboard lying on the stone-slabbed walkway. Didn't I change the plugs just before duck season? Sure I did. I remember changing the oil in the lower unit at the same time. Motor's OK; with a pat and a couple of pulls she'll purr like a kitten. What else now . . . let's see . . . shear pins. Don't forget them. Because of my innate ability to run an outboard onto the one strikable rock in any body of water, I invest heavily in shear pins.

Gas. I'll need new gas. The half a tank left from last fall must have collected some skip-sputter-stop condensation by now—worse than wet kindling. There was something else . . . oh yuh, a new primer bulb for the tank. Better pick up a couple of small hose clamps, too; fuel-line connections just love losing pressure. Boat's OK, registration's good until the end of the month so I'm legal for a couple of weeks, anyway. Trailer registration's good until August . . . hubs'll need a squirt of grease. Taillights. If I remember right they're shorted out—again.

As a flock of cedar waxwings fluttered among staghorn sumacs fuzzy with spring "velvet," my thoughts shifted to trolling tackle. I figure I have enough streamer flies to fool all the salmon in the state. Thanks to Frank Gray, my supply of needles for sewing on smelts will last until I make my last looping stitch. My tackle box holds miles of leader material, too many snap swivels, chain swivels, spoons, and a raft of lures whose names I can't remember. It also contains tools for the outboard. But unless my fishing partner is mechanically inclined, they amount to nothing more than a sham.

For once, my reels are ready. When hauling feathers, I'll use a Hardy wrapped with sinking fly line. For trolling smelts, it'll be a Medalist wound with two colors of lead-core spliced to 150 yards of backing. (Tell me *that* isn't the height of optimism.) Rods? I'm all set with a couple of old nine-foot sticks—one graphite, one 'glass—that I don't mind beating around in a boat.

After a cursory thought or two relating to a Thermos jug, bait bucket, life jackets, rain gear,

Toin Hennessey—

49

landing net, oars, extra spark plugs, etc., I allowed that I was prepared for this year's first open-water outing. But since the backdoor thermometer was getting redder in the face, I couldn't see any reason for discontinuing my cogitation.

With that, I made a mental cast toward May 1 and the opening of Atlantic salmon fishing. It brought an immediate double rise: buy an Atlantic salmon license and take my double-ender boat out to Fred Bean's place to be fitted with an anchor rig. Reflecting on salmon-fishing gear, I recalled replacing the backing on my reels last year and stopped there. To even consider a new rod, reel, line, etc., would have been totally ridiculous. Salmon flies? I've been tying them forever.

Sitting, almost snoozing, on the sun-warmed steps, I mused my way through May, June, and July without contriving a reason for accumulating more trout or bass-fishing paraphernalia. But August. Aaah, the backyard brimmed with the smell of ocean and images of bluefish. Then, I clearly remembered last year's promise to equip myself with a saltwater spinning outfit. What I want is a rod with enough muscle to heave a big plug or a rigged pogie, and a reel big enough to let a brawling blue know who's boss.

Abruptly, my morning mentation was interrupted by the sound of a vehicle pulling into the driveway. Directly, a door opened and closed, and seconds later my wife appeared on the walkway. "Well," she said, "I can see you've accomplished a lot this morning."

"You better believe it," I replied glancing at my watch. "In fact, I've mapped out a whole summer's fishing in a little more than an hour."

Apparently, only certain people realize there's more to sitting on the back steps than meets the eye—let alone what goes on in duck blinds and deer stands.

# Old-Timers

# Old-Timers

If I were asked what I like about old-timers, I'd say without hesitation, everything. Understand, that because I can no longer use the term, "middle-aged" without feeling somewhat pretentious, my reference to old-timers points to people who have reached the Biblical "three score and ten."

Personally, I think it's unfortunate that so many calendars are discarded before we begin to understand the meaning of the words, "the wisdom of the years." Naturally, that axiom relates to life in general, but nowhere is it more evident or true than in matters attendant to rummaging around in the outdoors.

In accordance with that—and I say this with-out disparaging my hunting and fishing part-ners—nothing pleases me more than sharing canoes and camps with men who have crossed more rivers and ridges than I'll ever see. I don't believe I'll ever grow tired of listening to them talk about old times but, aside from that, I like watching them. I like the slow, easy way they do things, and I never cease to marvel at how much they accomplish.

For example, ever watch an old-timer working up wood? Considering the size of the woodpile and his unhurried pace, you might think he'd be there until the cows come home. But he'll have that wood split and stacked in about as much time as it takes you to walk out to the mailbox and back. Keep in mind, too, that he probably paused to put an edge on the axe or to fill his pipe for a smoke. You can call it experience if you prefer, but the fact of the matter is you won't watch an old-timer going about his business for long without realizing he doesn't make any false moves; there's no backtracking.

So it is with hunting and fishing. An old-timer won't hurry to beat you to the next pool or the power line where the deer cross. Instead, he'll take his time, fishing purposefully or hunting diligently, and more often than not you'll regret that you didn't do the same. Also, why is it that,

Take It or Leave It

Summer School

even on a whitecapped lake, a canoe responds so willingly to the slightest twist or effortless push of an old-timer's paddle. Me? I could pull a muscle paddling across a millpond.

There's something quieting and calming about being in the company of old-timers. Maybe it's the individuality that seems to be lacking in today's younger generation, or the lines that years of living have etched into their faces, or the character in their eyes, or their open honesty and frankness. Whatever the reasons may be, I adhere strongly to the words I often heard during the time I was suffering growing pains: "Respect your elders."

Accordingly, whenever I see an older sport, somewhat stooped, perhaps, and with silver hair sticking out from under an old hat stained with sweat and insect repellent, I allow that I wouldn't mind having him in my canoe. In my mind, I see him as a tilting, graying, scraggly old spruce refusing to be pushed

off the bank of a stream by crowds of young and aspiring second growth.

It's a sure bet that if I were to take such an old-timer fishing he wouldn't be wearing the latest fashions from an outdoors-boutique business. To the contrary, I expect his attire would include a flannel shirt with an elbow either threadbare or gone, bleached and baggy chino pants, and patched

Tom Hennessey

rubber boots. No blousy fishing shirts or Velcro-pocketed pants or vests with the labels on the outside for my old-timer, no siree. Or for me, either.

And when he settled into the bow seat of my canoe, he'd talk fish and fishing: water levels and temperatures, phases of the moon, fly hatches, smelt runs, wind directions, which pools were filled in or gouged out by the spring freshet. This is stuff that makes sense to you and me but doesn't seem to matter to the flourishing crop of fly-fishing-school graduates who are more interested in where you bought your vest than they are in fishing conditions.

But not my old-timer. His tackle box would belong in the Smithsonian Institution. Antiques dealers would pay dearly for its contents. His rod? I'd say a hollow-glass Fenwick. His reel? A Pfleuger Medalist, no question. But regardless of his antiquated equipment, I wouldn't doubt for a second that he could sew on a smelt, fish a streamer, troll a lure, or cast a bass bug with the best of them.

All things considered, though, one of the things I like most about fishing with an old-timer is that when he gets a fish on, he doesn't yell, "Well all *right*!" or "Check it *out*!" or nearly roll the canoe over by hooting and punching the air with his fist. No, a man old enough to receive a free fishing license responds to a strike with, "That's more like it," or "It's about time," spoken quietly, of course, through a smile of satisfaction.

I have to say, however, that my respect for old-timers and my admiration of their unhurried and effortless ways are tarnished with envy. Not only did they see the best of Maine's hunting and fishing but they lived in slower, quieter, friendly times.

Unfortunately, I don't think that will be said about us when we're old-timers.

Streamers + Smelts = Salmon

## Streamers + Smelts = Salmon

"I hear they've been slapping them sideways with streamers," said the sport to his guide. Actually, the two were longtime friends and fishing partners. The fabricated distinction was determined by whose boat they used.

"You heard right," the guide answered as they walked onto the dock in front of his camp. Then, nodding toward the bait bucket the sport was carrying: "But I notice you made a stop at the bait shop."

"You bet," said the sport. "I'd rather fool 'em with feathers, but, to me, going spring fishing without smelts is like going bird hunting without a dog."

"It doesn't make a bit of difference to me what they take or if they take," the guide allowed, tugging at the visor of his hat. "You never know 'til you go. Besides, sometimes I get so comfortable out there I don't want to be bothered by a fish."

"Well, you won't be too comfortable today. Judging from this breeze, you'll have your hands full handling the boat. But don't worry, I'll do whatever I can to see that those salmon don't bother you."

"Oh, I'm sure you will," the guide replied as he fumbled in his shirt pocket. Directly, he stuck a cigarette into a tight-lipped grin and said, "Another nail in my coffin." With his back to the breeze, he tucked his head inside the opening of his jacket and lit the cigarette.

"Hell," said the sport. "You'll set yourself afire before those butts bury you."

"I hope so. One thing's for sure, I'm not going to worry about it. Now if you'll get aboard we'll see if these salmon are still sociable." The motor purred on the first pull and within minutes a Gray Ghost and a Supervisor followed the boat out of the cove.

"Good chop," the guide allowed as they trolled past the huge granite rock guarding the end of the point.

"Just right," the sport agreed. When the breeze nudged the bow, he advised, "Better step her up a little, keep these flies . . . Aha! Man, that didn't take long!" he exclaimed as his rod bucked and bowed.

Tom Hennessey —

"I told you they were taking," the guide said, his voice blending with the buzzing of the reel. "Nice fish, too," he noted as the cartwheeling salmon flashed silvery in the sunlight.

"*Was* a nice fish," the sport corrected. "He spit 'er out—quick release."

"No problem, we'll hook another one along here in no time," the high-spirited guide pre-dicted. Having heard that before, the sport smiled skeptically. But no sooner had he settled back in the boat seat when his Gray Ghost collided with another hit-and-run salmon.

What is it about trolling streamers for land-locked? Sure, it's about rods curved into cres-cents and reels beginning their recitals at high C. But it's more than that. It's about chilly after-ice-out air challenging the warmth of the spring sun, and about cloud shadows crawling over hills steepled with spruces and blushed with blossom-ing hardwoods. It's about the first pair of loons on the lake, and the chartreuse tints of alders and willows gathered at the outlet.

It's about rain squalls and windsongs and crows perched on pine stubs, missing nothing and broadcasting everything. And it's about an old leather fly book and the breezy-cool comfort of a boat brimming with friendship and springtime. Whatever it may be, trolling streamers for land-locks will always be Maine.

On that blue-bright afternoon, the guide and the sport had a grand time for themselves. Steadily, the landlockeds boiled and swirled at the streamers darting through the chop. Some were hooked, some weren't. Some were played and lost, others were boated and released. The sport kept one fish, a two-and-a-half pounder, to be broiled and served swimming in melted butter and chives.

A lot of laughter spilled from the boat as the two talked about old times—better times—and old friends, fishing and hunting, dogs, camps, anti-hunters, "do-gooders," women, kids, beer and whiskey, retirement, and places they planned to fish this spring.

Because they had such good luck on streamers, they switched to trolling smelts just for the heck of it. They hadn't left a hundred yards of wake when the sport felt a solid strike. At first he thought it was a togue. Seconds later, though, a brassy form broke the surface. "Bass," he said. "An old walloper, too."

When the fish was sculling beside the boat, the sport reached down and lifted it from the water by its lower jaw. Being an avid bass fisherman, he hefted the smallmouth, studying its length and depth. It would have come close to covering the blade of a paddle. As he released the bass he said, "That fish is on the heavy end of four pounds if it's an ounce."

The guide agreed. "This place is full of bass," he said, "Come down when they're spawning, and we'll fish them with poppers. It's a circus." He didn't have to say it twice.

During the next half-hour or so, the smelts never got a second look. Afternoon was edging into evening, and the boat seats were getting bumpy when the guide asked, "What do you think?"

"I think we ought to change back to streamers and troll back to camp. By the time we get there it'll be suppertime—that's if we're not bothered by any more salmon."

"I think you're right. But first reach in that cooler there, sport, and hand me one of those refreshments. A guide gets awful dry handling a boat in this sun and wind."

What is it about trolling streamers for landlocks?

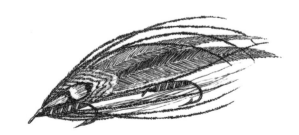

# Church of the Outdoors

## Church of the Outdoors

There's better than an outside chance that you and I are members of the same church. Although we will never be described as religious zealots, we are nonetheless devoutly conscientious about attending and supporting our place of worship.

An unusual church it is, to say the least. Nondenominational, devoid of dogmas, decrees, and hierarchies, its parish is boundless and its services are continual. Amid constant, often harsh displays of life and death, peace prevails there, as do comfort and contentment, honesty, and truth.

Not out of habit or fear do we remain faithful to our church, nor do we go there to pray for self-ish reasons or to ask forgiveness for being what we are. Never do we go there to be seen. We attend our church simply because that is where we feel closest to whomever or whatever God may be.

For those who are not yet privileged to be included in this parish, let me attempt to explain why the church that you and I attend is as wondrous and miraculous as the season at hand.

To begin with, awe-inspiring though they may be, the world's most magnificent cathedrals do not offer architecture more beautiful or intriguing than that of our church. Towering spruces and firs form its steeples and spires; its roof is a sun-streaked canopy of cerulean sky; and cloud-shadowed hills and mountains shape its domes and arches.

It would be impossible to imagine the forces that constructed its massive altars of granite and bent rainbows to form stained-glass windows and created chandeliers from the crystal-like castings of ice storms.

Most people will be surprised to know that our church's litanies are chanted by wild geese, and its hymns are sung by a choir of birds—accompanied, if you please, by the music of woodwinds. In its vestibules, baptismal fonts are formed by the waters of lakes and ponds spilling from immense bouldered basins. Ceremonial

Tom Hennessey —

and the smolder of autumn leaves.

In accordance with our church's unorthodox structure, the observance of holy days is not part of our unusual schedule. Instead, the arrival of each season is celebrated quietly but joyously.

Springtime, for example, is announced by the trilling of toads on evenings steamy with ground fog, by the buzzing of woodcock on thaw-spongy singing grounds, and, of course, by salmon fresh in from the sea.

Summer, the most festive of seasons, is celebrated with warm breezes, hazy sunlight, vibrant greenery, and fields cluttered with wild flowers. On inland waters, loons laugh at the aquabatics of kids at camp, and along the coast,

wines are fermented from the juices of fox grapes, blueberries, and elderberries, and incenses are fragrant with the aromas of wood smoke, grass fires,

fishermen practice patience as they wait for tides to fill silver bays and estuaries with runs of mackerel, blues, and stripers.

Autumn's arrival is marked by the pipings of teal and plover gathered in grassy coves, by a melon-colored moon coursing a sky frosty with stars, the chiming of dogs' bells, and by the whisper of wings in the dawn wind. And in deference to the inferno of foliage raging through hard-wooded hills, our church's altar is decorated with torches of scarlet sumac and tapers of golden hackmatack.

Soon thereafter, Ol' Man Winter arrives to seal lakes and ponds with ice-paned storm windows. To acknowledge his arrival, our church graciously changes its vestments to a seasonal white, as do the ermine and the snowshoe hare.

For the most part, the congregation is composed of wild creatures—or, more realistically, creatures considered wild because they fear man. Each of them, however, no matter how great or small, is equal in purpose and importance to a plan that we seem unable to understand.

Our church has no priests, but the lofty pines serving as its pulpits are religiously occupied by appropriately plumaged eagles. And because they are men who are blessed with wisdom and patience, old guides and grandfathers are the lectors

and ushers in the church of God's great outdoors.

With great reverence, we should regularly renew our vows to serve our church with respect, appreciation, and concern for its future, and we should welcome all who find the trail leading to it. Only by regular attendance and support will this sacred institution remain to be enjoyed by generations of parishioners who one day will have the privilege of passing this way.

# Much Obliged

# Much Obliged

In what seemed like a sigh from the setting sun, a warm breath of breeze ruffled the river.

"Man, it's humid, isn't it?" said Paul Reynolds as we slid the double-ender out of my truck and into the murky water. "I'll bet we'll have a hard time hooking a smallmouth tonight. They're probably all sweating this out around a springhole."

"If we had any brains, that's where we'd be," I replied while rattling the oarlocks into place. "But what the heck, I've never had any luck catching 'em at home and, besides, what we'll see here will be a lot more pleasant than what we'd see on the evening news."

"That's for sure," Paul agreed. "That's for damn sure."

What is it about stepping into a boat? That simple act seems to generate feelings of excitement, adventure, even magic. To me, it always feels like stepping off the edge of the Earth. Directly, I dipped the oars and the double-ender carried us into the humid haze shrouding the August evening. With a fly rod and a spinning rod in each end of the boat, plus the attendant tackle bags and boxes, we were ready to do business. All we needed were a few big-feeling bass.

"What'll we offer 'em first, poppers or spinning lures?" Paul asked.

"I'm starting with lures," I mumbled while rummaging in my tackle box. "I don't think we'll do much with poppers until the sun gets off the water." Fetching a soft-plastic, fluorescent-yellow lure from the box, I attached it to a jighead and predicted, "There, that'll do it."

"What d'you call that?"

"Mister Twister," I answered. "Pat Labree has been turning 'em inside out with it."

"The dog trainer?"

"That's him. When he gets tired of casting bird dogs, he casts one of these for bass."

"Well," Paul allowed as he snapped on a Jitterbug, "if you're fishing bottom, I'll fish on top."

Say, I didn't get two cranks out of my first cast when I felt a solid strike. Seconds later, a bass began our evening's entertainment with aquabatics that included cartwheeling leaps, tailwalking, and go-for-broke runs. With a shake of his head, my fishing partner thought aloud: "What scrappers they are. Unbelievably strong."

Lifting the "guesstimated" one-and-a-half pounder—a typical river smallmouth—from the water before releasing it, I agreed: "Right there," I said, "is a lightweight with a heavyweight's punch."

Glints of sunlight traced the arc of monofilament line when Paul made his first cast. It would be difficult to say whether the splash resulted from the plug's striking the water or a bass's striking the plug. It was that instantaneous. "How 'bout that!" the surprised angler ex-

claimed through the buzzing of his reel. "Looks like we're right in amongst 'em."

That we were, and we switched immediately to the sportier fly rods and popping bugs. So much for the sun's getting off the water. While an eagle soared in the smudgy sky and mallards called from darkening coves, we caught and released bass after bass. By the time we paused for a refreshment, we allowed that we'd caught a

Tom Hennessey

dozen or more and figured we must have lost that many to boot. Most of the fish were one-and-a-half pounders, give or take; a few were in the two-pound range. One we saw was bigger.

But after accepting Paul's invitation to our soiree, the patriarch of the pool changed its mind: Where a slow current spilled over a ledge, the water bulged as the big bass rose slowly—like an old dog climbing onto a couch—and took the popper with its back and dorsal fins showing. For an instant, the line tightened, but a moment later it fell to the water. "Quick release." Paul quipped around a smoldering Cigarillo.

Words never flow more easily than while fishing with a friend. So it was that we discussed people, dogs, hunting and fishing, politics, game wardens and biologists, fish and game laws, camps, filleting and cooking fish, boats and canoes—you name it.

A bat fluttered and swooped in the dusky dampness as Paul said, "I'm ready to call it quits whenever you are."

"One more and we'll head for the barn," I answered. We hadn't drifted far downriver when the sky's afterglow illumined the rings of a rising bass. Paul hooked it with one cast and released it shortly thereafter. By the time we reached the grassy slope that served as a boat ramp, the river was smothered with sweltering darkness.

Even the full moon's face was flushed with heat as it floated into the eastern sky. "That was good fishing," said Paul as we drove through the field and turned onto the dirt road. "Better than I expected in this weather. And you were right, what we saw was a lot more pleasant than what we'd see on the evening news."

That's for damn sure.

# The Eve of Opening Day

## The Eve of Opening Day

In a quiet corner of every fisherman's mind there flows the memory of a brook where, as a boy, he caught trout on opening day of fishing season. Chances are "your" brook was within walking distance of home. You may have reached it by hiking along the railroad tracks, a grown-up tote road, or by cutting across the pasture behind old man Curran's place.

There were times when you wallowed in snow as you fished its ice-embroidered pools and times when you slogged through a slurry of mud and cold spring rain. So it was that early on you realized the truth of the saying: "Fisherman's luck is a wet butt and a hungry gut."

But to a boy who'd been marking days off the calendar for a month or more, weather didn't matter one whit. You wouldn't have missed the first day of fishing season any more than you'd have missed the last day of school.

Fact of the matter is, you were probably less excited on Christmas Eve than you were on the eve of opening day. How many times did you extend the tip section of your steel telescoping rod that evening—making it just the right length for brook fishing? How often did you arrange your hat, boots, wool socks, and jacket by the back door, checking pockets for sinkers, snelled hooks, spinners, and, of course, your jackknife? And another drop of oil on your reel wouldn't do any harm, right?

Remember that reel? It had to have been either a nickel-plated Shakespeare, Bronson, Pfleuger, or J.C. Higgins. It featured a selective click drag that did or didn't, a level wind that would or wouldn't, and an "anti-backlash" label that was wishful thinking. A dented disc added a stutter to its tinny voice, one of its two handles was either split or missing completely, and the engraving on its side plates couldn't have been done with anything smaller than a roofing nail.

Being a fastidious fisherman, you checked and rechecked your line—a hand-me-down fly

70

A Break on the Barrens

First Come, First Served

line, no doubt, that wouldn't snarl or tangle as easily as regular braided linen—and you tested, then retested the loops connecting the line, spinner,

TOM HENNESSEY

and snelled hook. For sure, you changed the spinner from one of silver to one of gold several times.

In the cellarway, you checked once more the plastic bag containing the worms you dug from around the sink spout or over the septic tank. Next, you sliced a doughnut in two and stuck the circular halves together with peanut butter.

After wrapping it in waxed paper, you placed the sawdust-dry concoction in your hat so you wouldn't forget it. A drink from the brook, though, would sluice it down in good shape.

If opening day arrived on a weekend, you arrived at your brook about the time dawn was becoming daylight. Unfortunately, the long-awaited date usually occurred during the week, which meant that when school let out, you ran the mile or so to home in record time and fished in the afternoon.

There's no question that during a given season, you caught your share of trout, pickerel, bass, perch, and maybe a few stripers from the river. But no matter how often you wet a line, never was the excitement higher or the anticipation greater than when you approached that big-feeling brook on opening day.

Because of the high, cold water, you knew the fish would require some coaxing. Carefully, then, fishing slowly and thoroughly, you probed each pool, ripple, and run. Diligently, you followed the flash of the spinner as it disappeared in deep pools or was swept beneath undercut banks where doilies of foam decorated dark eddies. Lightly, you held the line as you listened with your fingertips for the slightest tap or tug.

Remember the names you gave the trouty places along your brook? "The Trestle," "Pitchfork," "Hemlock," "The Elbow," "Skunk Cabbage," "Two for Two," "Poison Ivy," and "Lunch Hole," among others.

You know as well as anyone that it was impossible to fish an opening-day trout brook without getting wet. Invariably, a bank would cave in beneath you, filling your boots with mud, snow, and spikes of frost. Always, you had to shuffle just a little farther onto a shelf of ice that you knew would hold you, and the best you could say for the hip boots that you at long last acquired was that they held more water than regular boots.

Chances are that by the time you set a course for home, the sun had dropped anchor for the night and the moon had left its mooring to go sailing among the stars. Pleasantly tired, cold, and powerfully hungry, you were, however, warmly

content with three trout that measured a tad more than eight inches apiece—if you looked at them long enough.

Now the only trouble with brooks is that they lead to bigger waters and bigger fish, which naturally tend to make a boy forget about small trout. Togue, salmon, and time have no doubt diminished your enthusiasm for thrashing around on brooks swollen and roily with spring runoff.

But, it's a good bet that the memory of your brook is flowing brightly in that quiet corner of your mind—and you can't help but wonder, if only for a moment, whether you could still catch a trout or two below The Trestle or down at Poison Ivy.

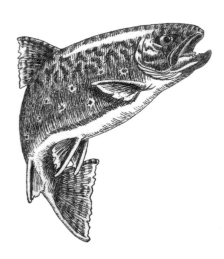

# The Christening

## The Christening

It was too nice a day for raking the lawn or going to the dump, so I did what any judicious man would do—I christened my new canoe. All I needed were paddles, a flotation vest, and a setting pole. No fishing equipment. It was too nice a day for concentrating on casting and retrieving. Too nice, even, for hooking and releasing fish. There's a time and a place for everything.

Now from what I've seen, I'm convinced that when the good Lord made the state of Maine, he had canoes in mind. If there's a better way to enjoy the endless miles of rivers and streams wandering through this neck of the woods, I've yet to find it. Better still, hereabouts you don't have to travel any distance to operate a paddle or a pole. Accordingly, within minutes after turning out of my driveway, I slid the glossy green seventeen-footer down a grassy bank leaning against a bridge on Black Stream.

Aside from a bird dog on a solid point, is there anything prettier than a canoe on the water? Pretty enough, for sure, to be referred to as "she." As lightly as a leaf, she floated in a quiet, foam-flecked eddy stained dark with the reflections of spruces. As the current gently nudged her, sunlight slid along each gunwale to collide in a silvery burst on her bow deck.

After placing a rock up forward for trim, I stepped into the canoe. Then, rocking it by shifting my weight from one foot to the other, I tested the stability of her thirty-six-inch beam. She was levelheaded, all right; from then on it would be up to me to keep her that way.

Responsive? You bet. Not once did she hesitate or object to a suggestion or command from the paddle. And because of her low profile, she wasn't swayed easily by the whims and coaxings of the wind. A good canoe, I'd say. Too good for me, my wife said.

In addition to those captivating qualities, the canoe was pleasantly quiet. So quiet, in fact, that she took me to within a few feet of a nesting

Canada goose. To my surprise and pleasure, the loudly honking bird rose from the swale to our right. After topping the greening willows, it scaled toward the stream and lit about thirty yards ahead of us. Only after careful scrutiny was I able to make out the well-concealed mound of grasses, mud, and weeds that was the goose's nest—and that I was content to leave alone.

Seconds later, the calling of a second Canada drifted along the stream. Directly, what I assumed was the gander came scaling toward us, low to the water. In a long, sliding splash, he joined his mate. Bobbing their heads and honking steadily, they swam ahead of us as I paddled slowly. Maintaining a distance of about thirty yards, give or take, the two geese appeared to be towing me and my quiet canoe.

Not until we were far along the stream did the pair's escalated honking signal that they were about to take wing. After lifting off and circling, they flew directly over us, returning to their nest.

The day was brimming with the sights, sounds, and smells of springtime. Where the stream narrowed into a marshy channel, I noticed that green roots were showing in last year's bleached-blond cattails. Sunlight spilling through a torn canopy of clouds silvered the wings of crows, and the perfumes of spruce and pine min-

gled with the pungent but pleasant odor of skunk cabbage.

The contrast in colors—brilliant greens, yellows, and maroons against darker greens—

was incredible. Funny thing about colors, Mother Nature can put them together any way she wants and they'll be nothing short of breathtaking. Unfortunately, it doesn't work that way in a painting.

In a narrow channel, the canoe waited patiently while I watched the subaqueous growth swaying gently to the slow rhythm of the current. Although insignificant and unimpressive in appearance, each moss, weed, stalk, and root is indispensable to the order of Nature—and to our lives.

Talk about the best things in life being free: While red-winged blackbirds spilled liquid notes on the marsh, a hatch of mayflies fluttered like confetti. When one of the delicate insects emerged on the surface close by, I lifted it carefully from the water with the paddle. While it perched, drying its wings, I changed the position of the blade in relation to the breeze. As the paddle moved, so did the mayfly—in the manner of a weathervane turning into the wind.

But enough sitting and paddling. When it was time to leave, I stood, leaned on "the cane," and turned the canoe toward the bridge. She glided easily with each push of the pole, and when I snubbed, she stopped willingly. We would go a long way together, that canoe and I.

Near their nest site, the geese were feeding in a bed of arrowhead. Alarmed, they swam to midstream. Then, honking and calling again, they led us toward the road. A short distance from it, they flushed and flew back. I wished them good luck.

After picking up the canoe and carrying her to the truck—she weighs only sixty-five pounds—I admitted that I liked her a lot and allowed that it was just as well I didn't bring a fishing rod along.

There's a time and a place for everything.

September Salmon

## September Salmon

Silvery wakes split the mirrorlike surface of the stream as the outboards purred us toward Hannibal's Crossing on the Penobscot River's West Branch. Here and there, shedding pines paled to tones of ochre, and ferns tinted orange flickered along banks bulging with alders. Scattered through the dark growth of firs and spruces, leaves of red and gold glowed like sparks from a fire.

After a swift lunch at Halfway House, we squirmed back into the canoes and set our minds to serious fishing.

A seam of orange showing in the leaden overcast suggested a Gray Ghost streamer. There was no shortage of salmon in the West Branch, but suffice it to say, they were not in a feeding frenzy. Between Halfway House and Big Island, where we rendezvoused to make camp, Don and I had several taps and tugs, but no reason to wet the landing net. So much for the Gray Ghost.

Just below Ragmuff, however, Larry landed a two-and-a-half-pound salmon and raised another. The secret, he allowed, was proper presentation. When the bow of Maurice's canoe grated on Big Island's gravel, he held aloft the twin to Larry's fish. Maurice claimed, however, that because he was a guide, his salmon weighed at least four pounds.

A soggy south wind chanted in the pines as we pitched our tents on the high-shouldered island. Soon afterward, the aromas of frying onions, green peppers, potatoes, and steaks mingled with the fragrance of wood smoke. A round of refreshments was served.

Oprah Winfrey would have gone off her diet for that dinner. And while the bright-eyed fire became sleepy-eyed embers, the conversation lingered on fishing, hunting, and the outdoors.

Next morning, after an unhurried breakfast of fried potatoes, scrambled eggs, and sausages made from caribou meat (from arctic Quebec), we loosened our belts and groaned into the canoes. Larry and Gary struck for upriver pools; Maurice, Seth, Don, and I drifted downriver.

In an eddy below Drive Camps, I felt a weighty tug that turned out to be an oversize chub. When we eventually drifted into The Foxhole, the landing net was still dry. The river's ribs were showing. Consequently, on the way back to camp the outboard clattered and bucked as we churned over rips and bars.

"From the way we're spinning our wheels," said Don, "I'd better get a new set of chains for that prop." If there's anything on God's green earth that would bother that joker, I've yet to hear of it. We never sheared a pin.

Maurice's canoe was anchored near Lone Pine, and as we approached, Seth held up a salmon that needed no measuring. "Took him right here," said Maurice pointing to the eddy boiling behind a large rock. "I lost another nice one earlier."

Gary also lost a keeper that morning. Nodding toward Larry, he said, "Don't ask how he did."

In answer to our questioning looks, the reply was, "Just a couple—it's all in the presentation." One, of course, was returned to the river.

"Tom," said my fishing partner, "you and I better scramble up over the bank and see if we can find something to change our luck." As it

turns out, we were followed. During a lunch consisting of sandwiches and steaming beef stew, we were visited by Eddie Speer, a fishery biologist for Georgia-Pacific. "They've seen a few flies," he said in regard to the salmon striking short, and he reported few big fish.

As for the afternoon's fishing, we would have done as well casting in the camp clearing. Darkness drizzled in early, and as we prepared a supper featuring salmon and bear steaks, rain drummed on the tarp we'd stretched over a spruce frame.

Bear steaks? You bet. Maurice supplied them and cooked them, and I'll say without hesitation, they were as good as any steak I've ever stuck a fork into. After trimming off the fat, the guide cooked them slowly in butter, green peppers, onions, and dashes of lemon juice to break down the meat's fiber. Testifying to his culinary skills was the fact that there wasn't a scrap of bear steak left when the meal was finished.

Talk about rain. During the night it came down so hard that if you stepped outside you had to hold your breath. Thanks to a tiny tear in one corner of our tent, Don, Seth, Maurice, and I spent the night in what could only be described as a swamp.

By late morning, remnants of clouds were dripping dry in a clearing west wind. Brooks were gushing and reaching long fingers of foam into the rising river as we made our final casts of the fishing season. Not a sign of a salmon.

It was late afternoon when we broke camp, loaded the canoes, and began the run back to Lobster Stream. Sure, the fishing could have been better; but what the heck, for three days we smelled the wood smoke, listened to the wind songs, and watched autumn coloring the West Branch country.

Fishing's only part of it.

# Pug

## Pug

Pug York was the last of the boat fishermen produced by the era that made the Bangor Salmon Pool a world-famous fishing ground for Atlantic salmon anglers. It was there, in fact, that our trails first crossed. As a teenager, I watched wide-eyed several times as Pug and Carroll Soucie of South Brewer hooked and played salmon in the tide-turbulent waters. Because I also lived in South Brewer, I now and then hitched a ride home with those accomplished outdoorsmen. That was during the early 1950s.

When dams and pollution eventually reduced the Penobscot's native salmon runs to nothing more than a memory, Pug directed his salmon-fishing abilities to the Narraguagus and Machias Rivers. Although he was an all-around fisherman who seemed to have a "magic touch" when it came to taking landlocked salmon, togue, and brook trout no matter where he fished, there was good reason that his heart never left the Bangor Salmon Pool.

As a young man, he guided fishermen at the Penobscot Salmon Club. "I got ten dollars a tide for rowing some of the older guys," he recalled. "I could row two tides in those days, so that was pretty good money." Obviously, he became addicted to *Salmo salar* at an early age.

To say that Pug knew the Pool from top to bottom would be abject understatement. But in addition to its traditional holding waters, he also knew several runs and pockets where salmon were comfortable at different points of the constantly changing tides. And he knew precisely when and how to present a fly to the finned aristocrats resting in those lies.

People who didn't know Pug were inclined to consider him abrasive and difficult to get along with. But I can tell you that his crusty, contentious demeanor was nothing more than a front. Actually, he was a sensitive, talented, extremely perceptive, and fiercely independent individual. I always figured his defensiveness was deep rooted and let it go at that, but I can say that if he considered you a friend, you had a friend indeed.

When Atlantic salmon returned to the Penobscot in the early 1970s, we became fishing partners. I wouldn't dare say how many hours Pug and I spent in a double-ender. But salmon are salmon, and as well as he knew those waters, we often fished for days without raising a single fish. When I'd grumble with discouragement, my partner would look over his shoulder and drawl, "Make another cast and keep fishin'." Shortly thereafter, though, would come this suggestion: "Wadda you say we haul ashore and have a couple of belts and see if that helps."

We fished in pelting rain, glaring sunlight, and wind that buffeted the boat and lifted our lines from the water. We caught some and lost some and had a lot of laughs in between. From experience, though, I learned that when Pug landed a

TOIII HENNESSEY —

salmon—he'd be so excited that I had to remove the fly—he was done for the day. Directly, he'd trudge up to the clubhouse where, after a couple of "quick ones," he recounted his success in detail to anyone who would listen.

Make no mistake about it, the man took his fishing seriously. When I got lucky and landed a salmon, say, on the morning tide, invariably I'd get a phone call that evening. "Aren't you a smooth article?" Pug would begin. Then, "Y'know, I saw that fish, too."

"So what," I'd answer, "I caught it." Naturally, our friendly competition sometimes ended in arguments. But again, the phone would ring later on and the same gravelly voice would ask, "We're still fishing partners, aren't we?"

When it came to fishing and hunting, Pug was superstition personified. For example, I once bought a Hardy "Marquis" reel for him during a trip to Montreal. When he realized the reel was a No. 2 model, he refused to fish with it. He was convinced that even numbers were a jinx. Accordingly, he once sold a deer rifle that his wife, Gloria, bought for him—its serial number ended with an even digit.

To me, regardless of all his idiosyncrasies, Pug was special. I valued his friendship and felt privileged to be his fishing partner. When he sold his prized two-handed Thomas rod to me—he built it when he worked for the prestigious Bangor company—I knew something was bothering him. But because he was such a private person, I didn't pry. When failing health eventually restricted his outdoor activities, which were, in fact, his life, he simply lost interest in living. During the last few years, he seldom left his house.

It disturbs me that I didn't respond to my mind's urging me to visit Pug on those frequent occasions when I thought about him. But it bothers me more that I was away at the time of his death and therefore missed his funeral. And it will bother me when I row my double-ender onto the Bangor Salmon Pool come springtime.

Farewell friend, and keep fishin'.

# Fishermen's Luck

## Fishermen's Luck

Each time there's a heavy rain, it reminds me of a day spent striper fishing at Bald Hill Cove, in the lower reaches of the Penobscot River. I had finished my junior year in high school and was the proud owner of an old square-stern canoe I bought from Carroll Soucie for ten dollars. Making the sixteen-footer even more of a bargain was the fact that it was rigged for rowing. The oarlocks I bought secondhand; the oars were given to me by "Bootch" Jamieson. They were long enough to row a Grand Banks dory; one was warped, and the other was bowed and had about two inches split off one edge of the blade. But what the heck, beggars can't be choosers.

After the canoe was patched and painted, and its bottom was shielded with orange shellac, my grandfather transported it to the South Orring-ton shore of the Penobscot atop his car. There was no public landing there at the time, only a dirt road that wandered through a field and ended in a grassy cove. The canoe spent the summer there. Oars and oarlocks contained within, it was left turned over behind a makeshift boat cradle that comforted an aging hull.

Because I didn't have a driver's license, my grandfather made quite a few trips to South Or-rington that summer. When he dropped me off at about six o'clock on the morning I remember best, the umbrella elms of the village were dripping rain. All the better. In addition to believing that fishing was best on rainy days, I had recently purchased a poncho at the surplus store. With that hooded, cape-like rain gear covering most of my hip boots, I figured I could stay dry standing under Niagara Falls.

With tackle box in one hand and fly rod in the other, I trudged down the muddied road to the river wondering why anyone would let a little rain rob them of a day's fishing.

No sooner had I rowed out of the cove when the leaking canopy of sky split a seam. In seconds, the ensuing downpour erased the shoreline reflections from the slate-gray river.

You've seen days like that: first it pours, then

Ready or Not

Double at Dawn

the sky brightens, then it pours harder. Several times I went ashore and dumped water out of the canoe. But the tide was rising, and the stripers—school fish from two to five pounds or so—were swatting my trolled streamer fly. And I was as dry as a duck—or so I thought.

Along about noon, however, I rowed into a shallow cove, shipped the oars, and reached for the sandwich I'd stuffed into the poncho's inner pocket. To my surprise, I discovered I was steamy with sweat. The poncho, nearly as wet inside as it was outside, had trapped the body heat generated by my rowing. Needless to say, the sandwich was somewhat soggy; even the wax paper had wilted. Nevertheless, it was a lesson learned. By the time I enlisted in the army I was well prepared for ponchos.

Sitting there eating my sandwich, I watched a shag, or cormorant, eat an eel. Between swallows, the bird would dip its bill and the flopping fish into the water. Then tilting its head upward, the

shag gulped with quick forward movements of its neck. The eel was consumed in less than a minute. Apparently, the shag dipped its bill in the water to facilitate swallowing.

The shores had taken all the shoving they could stand from the tide when I rowed back

onto the river. Directly, I set a course for the spindle buoy that marked a ledge below Bald Hill Cove. Approaching to within a few yards of the towering red beacon, I cast the streamer toward it and set the rod in my "rod holder," which was a stick jammed between the starboard gunwale and inner rail. With the rod propped against the stick and the reel butted against the tackle box between my feet, a striper usually hooked itself when it struck.

So help me, I hadn't taken more than three or four pulls on the oars when a fan-like dorsal fin appeared and a striper—let's say a bulky striper—took the fly in a bulge of water that I can still see. When I grabbed the bucking rod, which today hangs in my den, the reel was humming my favorite song. Unlike that of a school fish, the big striper's run wasn't swift. Instead, it was strong, steady, and unstoppable.

At the upper end of the ledge the fish sounded, and there it stayed. During the next half hour or so, I rowed above it, below it, and around it; I tried everything I ever heard of or could think of to move the fish, without results. Eventually I rowed out into the river, letting out all the fly line and most of the backing, and tried to tow the striper off its lie.

No such luck. The fish either was wrapped around a rock or had its fins braced in a crevice of the ledge. Thoughts of waiting for low tide were running through my mind when a blast that sounded like the fire horn at the Eastern Paper Mill took me about two feet off the seat. Emerging from the sheets of rain shrouding the river, an oil tanker was rounding the bend only a short distance upriver. Unloaded, it wasn't wasting any time heading out to sea. Let's just say that I didn't display any boyish bravado as the canoe towed a wake toward the Winterport shore. So long, striper.

By the time my grandfather picked me up that afternoon, I was convinced that the fish I lost weighed more than all those I caught. When I told him about breaking off the big striper because of the tanker he replied, "What a hell of a note!" Then, consummate gambler that he was, he added. "What do you suppose the chances would be of that happening?"

As I shed the clinging, clammy-wet poncho, I allowed that I didn't have the foggiest idea. I was wondering, though, what the chances would be of his driving me back to Bald Hill Cove the next morning.

Dunc

## Dunc

It's time I wrote about Duncan. In October 1988, my wife and I drove to a farm in Fairlee, Vermont, to pick a puppy out of a litter of Blackfield pointers. (You may know that these stylish bird dogs were brought to this country from Ireland by Dr. Rudy Winkelbauer of Brunswick, Maine.) When we arrived at the farm, the teenaged girl who answered the door said her father had been called away on business but that she would show us the puppies.

In a barn sweet with the smell of hay, we were greeted by a beautiful black-and-white pointer bitch and five equally attractive pups. Looking like spilled paint, the freckled-and-spotted youngsters scrambled toward us, excitedly tumbling and sprawling over each other. Directly, I was impressed by the alertness and responsiveness of a male that ran to me each time I whistled. The distinctively marked pup—a black mask covering his eyes and ears, two large spots on his rump—slept most of the way home and curled contentedly on our bed that night. My feigned objections were overruled by my wife.

The next day, owing to the pup's already obvious impatience, I named him Duncan of Blackfield, after my grandfather, the late Duncan L. MacDonald. Talk about a pup being full of promise. Dunc was a natural retriever and wasn't intimidated in the least by formal introductions to a cap pistol, .22 caliber rifle, and twenty-gauge shotgun, in that order. Better yet, the first time he inhaled bird scent—a pigeon planted in the field behind my house—he checked, stopped, and began creeping forward slowly, like a cat stalking a mouse. A tug on the check cord and a firm "Whoa!" stopped him. After steadying him with "good boy" praise while stroking his tail upward, I gently tried to push him forward and felt him stiffen and resist instinctively. At that moment, Rockefeller couldn't have bought him.

Naturally, Dunc was too young to hunt that fall, so I continued working him on planted birds.

Like any hunting dog worth its collar, he displayed intense desire. Moreover, he had a full-choke nose and was refreshingly tractable. Unlike most bird dogs, he wasn't averse to the command, "Here!"

Tom Hennessey

I began noticing, however, that after each training session Dunc appeared to be lame in his hindquarters. Thinking he might have pulled a muscle or ligament, I took him to the vet for examination and advice. When X-rays showed dysplasia in Dunc's hips, I felt as if the wind had been knocked out of me. There was no history of the disorder in the pup's breeding.

I was told the lameness would subside as Dunc grew but would recur when he matured. Accordingly, I was advised to hunt him sparingly and to treat his lameness with phenylbutazone, an analgesic used to relieve arthritis. "Don't worry, boy," I said to Dunc on the way home, "we'll deal with it."

On opening day of the next bird season, in less than half an hour of hunting, I shot the first three woodcock Dunc pointed. Finding birds that quickly was, of course, pure luck. But as luck would have it, that hunt turned out to be the beginning of a pattern that continued for the next four years. During short hunts in "easy covers"— mostly edges and corners—Dunc usually found enough birds for me to bag a couple to bake with the beans.

Eventually, though, it became obvious that the classy pointer's hunting days were numbered. When progressive lameness became a penalty for Dunc's pleasure, I retired him. Even though his spirit would have sustained him in the field, I wasn't going to watch the dog suffer for the sake of a few birds.

To compensate for Dunc's misfortune—it was like seeing an outstanding athlete's career cut short by a debilitating disease or an accident—I made him my constant companion. In addition to becoming a regular passenger in my pickup truck, he snoozed on couches and chairs in my den while I wrote or painted—always keeping one eye on me and the back door. While I worked, he would often groan repeatedly until he got my attention. Then, with his chin resting on the arm of his chair or sofa, he would look at me and wag his tail as if to say, "Y'know, this retirement isn't all that bad." Still, I felt like a traitor when I had to leave him behind during hunting season.

The cancer that took Dunc's life early this spring seemed to occur all at once. Like a pot boiling over, it had simmered slowly until spilling with alarming abruptness. When Dunc first began limping on his left front leg I wasn't overly concerned. He had done that in the past, and aspirin gave him relief from what I thought was probably arthritis. But when he continued limping, stopped eating, and spent his days lying lethargic on the den couch, I took him to the vet. X-rays revealed a sarcoma in his left shoulder and spots on his lungs.

It was too much, too late. Shortly thereafter, my wife and I were up all one night with Dunc, taking him outside. He was deathly sick, weakened from vomiting and diarrhea. When the latter showed blood, I knew the time had come to do what was best for the dog. Early that

morning, with the vet's assurance that I had made the right decision, Duncan of Blackfield went to sleep in my arms.

Unabashedly, I'll say Dunc's passing caused me unusual grief. He was special for a lot of reasons: a gentle, easygoing nature that belied his toughness; the playful way in which he accepted "Pete," the English pointer pup that inherited his bell; his comical impatience and persistence in letting me know precisely what he wanted, including the chair I was sitting in. And I always gave it to him. What are friends for?

Allowing that life, at its longest, is short, I removed Dunc's collar and bade him good-bye with: "Hunt on ahead, old boy. I'll catch up with you in a while."

# Spirit of the Season

## Spirit of the Season

Tell me you haven't noticed the gold-leaf finish on poplars, or the stains of purple asters spreading through fields brassy with goldenrod, and I'll tell you I haven't noticed the dew glistening rimy on moldering gardens or swamp maples blushing on the rims of bogs. Let's face it, lies of that magnitude should be left to the likes of Saddam Hussein. The truth of the matter is you and I are more than aware that autumn has arrived and hunting season is just over the hill.

Personally, I see autumn as a magnificently arranged parade marching to crescendos of color, signaling that the season of guns and dogs and deer camps is at hand. And the more I see of it, the more I realize that the heart and soul of the time-honored tradition of hunting are embodied in the spirit of the season.

Tell me I'm wrong: There'll be icicles hanging in hell when you're as enthusiastic about painting the back steps as you are about slapping a coat of olive drab on the canoe or duck boat. Likewise, when it comes to getting things ready for fall, the hunting camp takes precedence over the house, and people who wear panty hose notice their spouses—who can't remember trash day—studying tables listing tides and legal shooting times.

You yourself have probably observed that when you're taken by the spirit of the season—and a touch of Yankee frugality—the distances to gun shops located in outlying towns becomes shorter. Bagging a season's supply of steel shot at two bucks less a box is well worth the drive, the price of gas notwithstanding.

I admit to being hit with a magnum charge of boyish excitement whenever I walk into sporting-goods stores where the spirit of the season is as bright as fireweed. I like the gleam of lights on gun stocks and barrels, the smell of Hoppe's No. 9, and the racks of blaze-orange clothing glowing like the leaves of staghorn sumacs. And no matter how much I resolve to purchase only a hat or gloves, it's a sure bet I'll head for the barn with another duck call, two more bandannas, additional bootlaces, spare flashlight batteries (if not a flashlight), a can opener that a lot of us were introduced to via U.S. Army K-rations, a first-aid kit, a dog bell or two, probably a whistle, and, of course, one more blaze-orange dog collar. The adage "A fool and his money are soon parted" may apply here, but what the heck, no one ever saw a hearse stop at a bank.

Simply put, the spirit of the season overwhelms me. I like fussing with my hunting gear and thinking that what I'm doing will really make a difference—tacking a piece of leather to the sculling oar, for example, to eliminate chafing or rattling that might spook ducks, and attaching wheel weights to the tip of its blade to keep it submerged. Another ritual is readying a Great Blue Heron "confidence decoy," used to convince trafficking ducks that the coast is clear. Shy and reclusive, herons don't take kindly to human activity. With

such devices in store, I smugly allow that the stage is set for opening day. Trouble is, though, the ducks don't always read the script.

Nevertheless, I like checking out tips on trails leading to inland marshes and coastal coves where teal arrive early, and black ducks and whistlers stay late. I like the sounds of the north wind sighing in

Tom Hennessey —

the eaves at night, snow whispering at the window in the wee hours, and a Labrador retriever grunting "get up" long before the alarm goes off.

I'm honored to be sworn to secrecy when shown a clean-bottomed woodcock cover moist with spring seeps, and I like the feeling of reciprocation. Most assuredly, I anticipate the abrupt, magical silence of a dog's bell, shouting "Bird!", and the smell of gunpowder mingling with the cidery scent of autumn. But I have to say I enjoy hunting and the spirit of the season more than the shooting. It comes with age.

The passing years, however, will never change the feelings I have when I stop by old covers, places that are either grown up and gone by or where hunting is no longer legal because of residential development. They help me to whistle up images of my dogs Snooky, Misty, Jake, Sam, Coke, Dunc, and the special days and seasons we shared. Nor will time ever tarnish the memories of old hunters who taught me lessons and values that are as clear today as tracks on snow.

Frankly, I can't think of anything that I don't enjoy and appreciate about the spirit of the season. I like talking with farmers and wishing I had their hands-on knowledge of the land. I like the quiet, cordial ways of country folk and the clutter of village stores, where Maine accents and expressions are priceless. And I absolutely love it when a parent tells me that a son or daughter has tagged a deer for the first time.

If your autumn attire leans toward brush brown or camo early on and blaze orange later on, you know the time-honored tradition of Maine hunting arrives with the dawn of opening day. So, toss a treat for the dog into the pack basket and enjoy the spirit of the season.

# The Maple Syrup Fly

## The Maple Syrup Fly

"Ever heard of the Maple Syrup fly?" Jay Robinson asked as we pulled into the parking lot of a variety store in Medway.

"Can't say as I have," I answered. "Must be a local pattern."

"You won't believe it when you see it," said the master Maine guide. "If they've got any left, that is. It's a killer."

*Another killer fly,* I thought as we entered the store. But when the woman behind the counter greeted Jay with, "I know what you're after, and if there are any left you're lucky," my skepticism dropped like a snagged backcast.

"Just right, two apiece," said Jay as he fetched the last of the Maple Syrups from a display case containing Alvin Theriault's exquisitely tied trout flies. Let's just say that, although I prefer sparsely dressed patterns, I was taken aback. Wrapped to the No. 12 long-shank hooks were bodies of tan chenille, tails of yellow mohair—and nothing more. No wings, no hackles, no ribbings, nothing. "Don't laugh," Jay cautioned. "You'll be sorry."

Cloud shadows climbed Mount Katahdin as we drove to Jay's father's camp on the West Branch of the Penobscot. Situated between Abol and Pockwockamus Falls, "Wiggie" Robinson's woodsy retreat looks the mile-high mountain smack in the face. While admiring the altar-like magnificence of the landmark that was sacred to Maine Indians, ethereal to Thoreau, and esteemed in story and song by West Branch river drivers, I realized again why the Katahdin region is referred to as "God's country."

After an enjoyable dinner of barbecued chicken, the mid-afternoon sun signaled that it was time for Wiggie, Jay, and me to take the trails leading to back-of-beyond trout ponds.

As the crow flies, the canoes were stashed about three miles from where we left the truck. As a man walks, however, the distance was closer to four miles. Because the trail was mostly downhill, our packs seemed light and the miles passed quickly as we talked about fishing, hunting, bird dogs, outdoors writing—you name it.

On leaving the trail, we followed moose tracks through woods sweet with the smell of wild raspberries. After paddling across a small pond whose jade-tinted water sparkled jewel-like in the breeze, we lugged our gear over a ridge that rose above the ponds we were to fish. Directly, we rigged our rods and launched two canoes—Jay in one, Wiggie and I in the other.

Suffice it to say, the breeze that was a blessing during the steamy walk-in quickly became a curse. Consequently, we spent more time positioning and anchoring the canoes than we did fishing. Shortly thereafter, my undaunted guides allowed that we'd do better elsewhere. Without hesitation, we went ashore and dragged the canoes through the mire of a stump-studded bog that brought us to the smaller, wind-sheltered pond.

By the time Wiggie and I dropped anchor, Jay—who started fishing only a minute or so ahead of us—was playing a trout that took a Maple Syrup fished deep. Following suit, my second cast with the same pattern produced a fourteen-inch brookie with copper-toned flanks and fins the color of fireweed. Not to be outdone, Wiggie wasn't long

in landing a keeper (ten inches was the minimum legal length) and losing another. A while later, I landed two more trout that were released because they required measuring. It seemed, though, that Jay's rod was dancing a jig whenever we looked his way. He must have caught eight or ten trout,

but he kept only a couple—all on the oh-so-sweet Maple Syrup fly.

When the breeze began sighing a farewell, we dragged the canoes back through the bog to the bigger pond. Come dusk, the green drake (mayfly) hatch would emerge, providing an opportunity for dry-fly fishing. No sooner did we anchor in a cove where a spring brook spilled into the pond when a green drake as big as a butterfly fluttered into the air. While Wiggie changed to a floating line, I cast the Maple Syrup and immediately had a hard strike that came unstuck. During the hatch, trout continued to take the local favorite, which apparently resembled a green drake nymph rising to the surface.

Likewise, Wiggie's dry fly had hardly settled to the surface when a trout slurped it hungrily. Across the cove, Jay was playing a fish, too. And so it went. The craggy face of Katahdin was rouged by the setting sun as we caught, kept, and released wild trout (voluntarily and otherwise) while bats swooped and dove around our canoes, delighted with the arrival of dusk and the fly hatch. Small wonder that, when the mountains were veiled with mist wraiths, it occurred to me that I was seeing the breath of God.

When we packed up our gear, we had a total of eight trout averaging eleven inches, give or take. The daily limit was five per angler. Making

sure nothing was left behind, we began the steep walk out beneath a sky frosty with stars.

Now, I'll say that if the good Lord lets me live to a ripe old age, I hope I can walk in Wiggie Robinson's tracks. The man is seventy-six years old, and not once during the muscle-stretching, lung-pumping, heart-laboring hikes into and out of the trouty hinterlands did he say, "Let's slow down" or "Let's take a break." To the contrary, he set the pace. Nor did Wiggie shirk dragging the canoes or paddling, and—without exaggeration—his catlike quickness and agility were truly remarkable. Simply put, I was impressed.

From start to finish, every aspect of that trout-fishing trip was pleasurable, invigorating, productive, and—of course—memorable. But to sum it up succinctly, I would describe our outing in God's country as distinctly, traditionally, and wonderfully Maine.

# Triple Play

# Triple Play

I'm not bashful about saying that my birth certificate is stamped with the state of Maine seal. Moreover, I don't hesitate to say that in the travels that have been my privilege and pleasure, I have yet to make camp in a place where I would rather live. But because that statement is sure to raise a few eyebrows, I offer three anecdotes, each of which occurred recently during a single day's fishing. I think they might explain why I never "pulled up stakes," as they say.

Perhaps you know that a little rain to sweeten the river is all that's needed to put an Atlantic salmon fisherman's feet on the floor before daylight. Toss in a high tide at midnight and an increasing trap count in the fishways at the Veazie Dam and you have the reason I drove to the Penobscot's Eddington Shore Pool during a predawn downpour.

Now, you'd think a man who had cast flies to Atlantic salmon for more than forty years would be the exemplar of the adage, "Never be in a hurry to catch a salmon, because seldom is a salmon in a hurry to be caught." But if you know the difference between a Blue Charm and a Green Highlander, you know that's not the case.

Haste, however, makes waste.

In the parking lot above the Eddington Shore, where the land slopes toward the river, I hurriedly flipped the truck's transmission into "Park," or so I thought. Actually, the shift lever dropped back into reverse, which held the truck in place while the engine idled. Leaving the headlights on, I got out of the cab, sorted out my gear, and squirmed into chest-high waders.

In my eagerness to secure a place in the pool's rotation—a half-dozen or so anglers already had rods in the rack—I quickly switched off the lights and reached over the steering column to cut the engine, without realizing that I had nudged the gearshift into neutral. In the next instant—and to my total surprise—the truck was rolling toward the river.

Talk about your coffee being curdled. Throwing my rod and tackle bag aside, I sprinted—

Katahdin Country

Leap for Liberty *from the collection of Richard J. Warren*

108

wearing waders, if you please—and with a move that would be the envy of an Olympic gymnast, dove into the cab and arrested the runaway vehicle. After untangling myself from the steering wheel and four-wheel-drive shift lever, I expelled a long sigh of relief that steamed the windshield. Afterward, my fishing partners and I joked about their sport nearly being interrupted by a pickup truck's plummeting over the bank and into the pool.

But the best of this anecdote was yet to come. Shortly thereafter, while swimming a No. 6 Green Highlander through the pool, I hooked, landed, and released a salmon that was as fresh as the falling rain. What a way to start a day.

By noon the sun was casting short shadows, and I was in a canoe casting fly-rod poppers for smallmouth bass. Where a deep cove dented a gravelly shoreline, the deer-hair patterns agitated the spawning bass into one brawl after another. And nice bass they were—scrappy two-and-a-half and three pounders, with one going a strong three-and-a-half.

There's more to fishing, though, than catching fish. I was casting near a point of ledge when a deer—a doe, I reckoned by her trim figure—came out of the woods and began browsing on shoreline vegetation. Upon noticing me, she abruptly lifted

her head, cocked her ears forward, and stood taut, like a spring ready to uncoil. It was a picture to be painted: Illumined by sunlight, the deer's reddish-brown coat and the verdant grasses glowed against the deeply shadowed woods beyond. The contrasting colors were dramatic.

Apparently, the doe figured I was no cause for alarm. After feeding awhile longer, she turned and walked casually into the woods. While I admired the silence of her departure, something struck the water behind me with startling force. *Beaver,* I thought as I turned to look. But to my surprise I saw an osprey lifting off the water with a fish in its talons. The usually man-shy "fish hawk" made its explosive power dive so close by—about forty feet away, give or take—that I was able to identify its prey as a yellow perch. As I paddled around the point, it occurred to me that I must not cut what is commonly referred to as "an imposing figure."

Because I ascribe wholeheartedly to the saying, "Time and tide wait for no man," I struck for a striped-bass stronghold in an estuary of the Penobscot River on that evening's ebbing tide. Where a long finger of gravel tickled the current into laughter, the lightweight schoolies hit trolled lures and cast bucktail jigs with heavyweight punches.

What is so rare as a day in June?

A day of unforgettable fishing experiences.

I was playing one striper when several fish, obviously spooked, broke water ahead of a sudden, surging wake that rocked the boat. Seconds later, a seal surfaced between me and the shore. I figured that was the end of my fishing but, surprisingly, it wasn't. Even though the seal stayed in the vicinity, I continued catching and releasing stripers until the surrounding hills were silhouetted in the deepening dusk.

Running at a full gallop, the ten-horse outboard towed a wake toward the boat landing. Beneath a sliver of moon, a squadron of cormorants winged overhead like bombers on a night mission, while swallows—swooping and diving like fighter planes—attacked swarms of insects rising from the river. In admiring the beauty and serenity of the scene, it occurred to me that the day's outstanding fishing and attendant anecdotes had produced a limit of sound reasons for never pulling up stakes.

# A Matter of Time

## A Matter of Time

There wasn't a hint of dawn in the drizzling darkness, and the fog on the lake was thicker than smoke from a smudge. As I rummaged for the flashlight that had rolled off the boat seat, my son, Jeff, said in a hushed voice, "Listen . . . hear 'em?" At the far end of the lake, geese—a lot of geese—were gossiping.

"They must be getting ready to take off," said Jeff, still keeping his voice low.

"I don't think so," I answered. "Geese usually don't fly until well after daylight, later than ducks. We might get a chance at them when they head for the cornfields. Usually, they go out over

where we'll be set up—what're you whispering about, anyway? Get Magnum in here; we're wasting time."

The boat rocked as the big Labrador came aboard. Seconds later, the ten-horse outboard pushed us through the pitchy smother at half throttle. When the murky silhouettes of spruces emerged from the fog minutes later, I cut the motor. So far so good—the volume of goose music was louder.

By the time we rigged whistler decoys off a small point, set a few phony black ducks in the marshy cove, and hauled the boat behind a stand of cedars, we were sweating. "Can you believe this weather?" asked Jeff as we settled into a brush blind.

"Softer than a wool sock," I allowed. "Dead air, too; not exactly duck hunting weather. Better start off with No. 2s. If we do business early, it'll be with ducks. Take these BB loads, though," I said, handing him three shells. "When those geese start getting edgy, switch over."

Shortly after daylight, the rush of air through primary feathers sounded like cardboard being ripped. "Ringnecks!" I exclaimed as the swift-flying ducks vanished in the swirling vapor. The sound alerted Magnum. With cocked ears and excited eyes he glanced from Jeff to me. Half an hour later, he was still glancing, and the geese were still gossiping.

"Doesn't look good," Jeff thought aloud. "Should be more ducks moving by now."

"Well," I replied, "let's try the old coffee trick. That usually brings something scaling in." While we sipped the steaming brew, Jeff continued staring into the fog. "Don't worry about those geese," I began, "They'll . . ."

"Watch it!" Jeff nodded to my right. So long, coffee. Low to the water, a black duck came straight at the decoys. Suddenly, though, it lifted and veered. When I fired, the duck fell into the bog behind us. After minutes of thrashing, swimming, wallowing, and lunging in a hellhole of stumps, heath bushes, and cattails, Magnum found the nice black and delivered it to Jeff.

"There's the reason duck hunters should never leave home without a retriever," I said. "We never would have found that bird."

Talk about being singleminded: Jeff was still thinking aloud about the flock of Canadas. "Those geese didn't get up when you fired. Next thing you'll tell me is there's an old gander out there wearing a watch."

"OK," I said. "But I'm telling you, these birds operate on a schedule."

During the next half hour or so, the fog lifted as we listened without interruption to the chorus on the lake. But when the geese abruptly stopped

ToмHennessey —

113

clamoring, the silence was stiff with warning. Quietly, we switched loads. Directly, the geese began swimming down the middle of the pond. Eventually, a raft of about five hundred was strung out in front of us—an avian armada taxiing to a takeoff point. "Jeff," I whispered, "if you move I'll cut you out of my will."

Seldom do large flocks of geese take wing all at once. When the first gaggle lifted off—their cries rivaling the cheers of a Super Bowl crowd—they swung to our left. But the next geese came straight at us in two groups, one behind the other. The first bunch gained just enough altitude. "Let them go, Jeff," I said. "The next group's lower."

God, they were big. On they came, honking, yelping, grunting, and piping, their wings pumping. "OK," I said, "now or never." When my shotgun jolted my shoulder, the object of my attention folded and fell into the woods near a scrawny hackmatack. Magnum and I charged off in that direction. Minutes later, dog and goose collided in a weave of alders and willows. Mag wasn't long in settling the dispute, though, and again he ignored me as he lugged the biggest bird he had ever fetched out to his life-time hunting partner.

"Did you knock one down, Jeff?" I asked when I returned.

"If I did it hasn't struck yet," he answered.

"The way that one came out of the air I figured we were shooting at the same bird," I allowed. The air was filled with the wonderfully wild calls of geese as the majestic waterfowl winged toward nearby cornfields to feed. When things quieted down I looked at my watch.

Noticing me, Jeff said, "Seven o'clock, right?"

"Nope," I answered with a shake of my head. "Twenty after. These dark mornings delay them a little."

It didn't matter that we never fired another shot. Whenever you go duck hunting and come home with a Canada goose you can call it a great day—especially in weather softer than a wool sock.

TOM HENNESSEY —

# Fiddleheads and Black Flies

## Fiddleheads and Black Flies

When we came ashore from fishing Brewer Lake, my son, Jeff, was having second thoughts: "I should have kept that salmon I released to have with the fiddleheads I picked yesterday."

"Well, when you caught that one and then lost another right off quick," I replied, "I figured we were right in among 'em." But not a tap or a tug did we have in the next three hours—even after changing from streamers to smelts.

"How's the fiddlehead crop?" I asked as we loaded the boat onto the trailer.

"Pretty good. I didn't spend much time picking a six-gallon bucketful, anyway. I had some

that night with a piece of haddock—I'd rather have had brook trout or salmon, but fillet of fresh haddock's not too shabby. Give those fiddleheads a day or two and there'll be another crop ready."

"Sounds good to me. I've had a hankering for something fresh doused with vinegar, and I don't mean dandelion greens." Two days later, beneath a sky as blue as a robin's egg, my oldest offspring and I followed the rippling music of a woodland stream celebrating springtime.

Here in Maine, the gifts of April and May are special. Think about it, you can dip smelts and fish for Atlantic salmon and striped bass in rivers that run right through towns. You can start a brawl with a smallmouth bass by casting a popping bug from a canoe, hook a landlocked salmon with a trolled streamer, tempt trout with dainty dry flies on back-of-beyond ponds or flowages, and pick a mess of fiddleheads along a brook handy to home. Those are gifts that matter, which is why so many people are striving so hard to protect them.

For the benefit of first-time fiddleheaders, the clean, dark-green stalks and curled heads grow in tightly knotted clusters that are easily distinguished from the paler and fuzzier features of common ferns. Another identifying feature of fiddleheads is the flimsy casing that covers each sprout. As it unfurls—it's as thin as an onion skin and similar in color—this casing breaks, but usually remains attached.

Tom Hennessey

Jeff was right. A new crop was growing among the stubble left from his first harvest. As we picked beneath a lacy canopy of leafing hardwoods, I noticed that some of the fiddleheads were sunburned and the soil was dust-dry in spite of spring's cold, wet weather. The combination of steady winds and the thirst of trees leafing out had dehydrated the land, leaving the woods as dry as kindling.

Within half an hour or so, the six-gallon pail held about five gallons of fiddleheads. Considering that the black flies also had blossomed, I allowed that five gallons was enough for me to clean.

Funny thing about black flies: At times they'll swarm around you and not bite, but at other times they'll attack every piece of exposed skin that isn't lacquered with insect repellent. As long as we were moving, the bugs were bearable. But whenever we stopped to pick, we paid an unholy penance. We literally breathed the black clouds that erupted from the disturbed ground cover. As usual, one went straight down my windpipe and left me retching and gagging until I thought I'd toss up my toenails. It isn't springtime until you swallow a black fly.

As we hustled along the stream toward the trail, I asked, "Are there any trout in here, Jeff?"

"A few, but there'll be more later. It seems that they go into the brooks early and then drop back in later on. I've caught some nice ones here."

Prettier trout water would be impossible to paint. Here, a rock-studded run was dark with the reflections of spruces; there, eddies were flecked with foam; beyond, riffles were silvered with sunlight. As you might expect, long-fingered ledges now and then tickled laughter from tranquil flows. The umber-toned bottom was a mix of fine gravel and rocks of all shapes and sizes. It looked, sounded, and smelled trouty—you know, the mingled aromas of skunk cabbage, mud, and the musk of bog. It would be a proper place to catch a brookie.

As we trudged toward the truck, parked in a field, I planned on fiddleheads for supper. I could taste them seasoned with salt, splashed with vinegar, and served with a mound of fried-to-a-golden-brown smelts. The rest of the greens would be blanched, bagged, and frozen to accompany later meals of steamed salmon with egg gravy, fried mackerel, charcoal-broiled bluefish, and—the good Lord willing—a few copper-bellied brookies. We don't make much money up here in Maine, but we don't go without much, either.

After dropping Jeff off at his place, I stopped alongside a hillside pasture dotted with a small herd of cows. Naturally, they all stared at me while I gazed across the blossoming landscape. As far as I could see, softly blended greens, maroons, grays, and yellows were accented with the white bursts of apple blossoms. Like washes of watercolor paints, the springtime palette eventually dissolved into the blue haze that shrouded the distant hills. In the farmyard, a girl was coaxing a cat out from under a tractor, and in the field beyond, two boys and a dog explored a brook.

As I pulled back onto the road and headed for home, I allowed that there might be a better place than Maine for appreciating springtime, but I doubted it.

A Monument to Misty

## A Monument to Misty

Maybe you know what I mean when I say old bird covers remind me of abandoned cemeteries found way back in the hills. Surely you've discovered one or two in your time: moss-mantled stones grown over with briars and hardhack bush, and cluttered with the bones of biomass.

The stone walls that stumble through old covers, of course, are not inscribed with names to read and possibly recognize. Yet, those familiar tangles of alder and poplar "grown up and gone by," as we say, are grand monuments to great dogs whose names are etched forever in our minds. Accordingly, I stop by an old cover every now and then and pay my respects to a dog named Misty.

Oddly enough, the birdy Brittany spaniel came into my life through a stroke of fisherman's luck. On a June morning in 1961, Frank Gilley and I were fly fishing for striped bass in the Bangor Salmon Pool. Between strikes, we hooked onto the subject of bird dogs. Frank was feeding four "feather hounds" at the time. I, however, was dogless because my hunting partner of fourteen years, a springer spaniel named Snooky, had flushed her last bird the previous fall.

"Y'know, I've got a Brittany you might be interested in," Frank offered. "I have too many dogs now, and, besides, she killed a couple of my turkeys. She's about two years old and has a lot of potential. If you want her, you can have her." Shortly thereafter, we set a course for Frank's "Tip-Top Farm" on Copeland Hill.

When Misty burst from the kennel, her bobbed tail was a blur as she bounded toward me smiling, sneezing, and wiggling for all she was worth. Then and there the beautifully marked liver-and-white Brittany owned me. Typically spaniel, Misty was gentle, friendly, and full of hunting instinct, which she displayed in short order.

Our first stop after leaving Frank's place was Ring's gravel pit, on the Field's Pond road. At that time, pheasants occupied the sprawling fields, acres of feed corn, and brushy hedgerows bordering the pond. In an open area of grass rimmed with alders, Misty began making game almost immediately. Seconds later, she locked into a solid point. And so did I, mesmerized by the magic of a pointing dog—mine—paralyzed with bird scent. When I came to my senses and walked in ahead of her, a hen pheasant flushed and flew toward the swale edging the pond. So began twelve years of bird hunting the likes of which I'll never see again.

Because I was working nights then, Misty and I hunted nearly every day of bird season, regardless of weather. Now, if you were wearing bibs instead of shooting vests back in the '60s, believe me when I say that birds—particularly woodcock—were plentiful. And covers were close by. Seldom did I hunt more than fifteen miles or so from Bangor, where I lived at

the time, and seldom did I return home without a mixed bag of woodcock and partridge. It seemed that every edge and corner of cover held birds.

Simply put, hunting with Misty was pure pleasure. She worked close, handled easily, had a full-choke nose, was stiff as starch on point, and retrieved naturally. She once swam to fetch a black duck I shot after it flushed from a beaver flowage in Glenburn.

To this day, I have never hung a bell on a dog

with more heart and desire, and I've owned a few. Misty would barge out of the dog box in late afternoon with as much enthusiasm as she did when the covers were fuzzy with frost in the morning. Once, after Frank Gilley and I had bagged a double limit of woodcock over her, the now-retired orthodontist praised the hard-hunting spaniel: "Misty, old girl, you sure know your business. I should have spent more time with you."

Frank usually hunted behind setters and pointers. Subsequently, however, he followed the bell of a Brittany named Andy. Maybe the veteran sportsman saw something in Misty. And maybe that something moved him to say this fall—the first time he was dogless in more than fifty years—"Come springtime I think I'll start looking for a Brittany spaniel."

Time, of course, is a tyrant. Eventually, the years took their toll on the little dog that so graciously taught me everything she knew about birds. By then, however, I had put a collar on an English pointer pup named Jake. Naturally, the newcomer provided Misty a well-earned rest, but she didn't appreciate it in the least. Although she ached with the infirmities of old age, her heart still yearned for what was her life and love.

It was springtime—June, in fact, the same month she came bounding into my life—when Misty went to sleep in my arms. Admittedly, on the way to the veterinarian's office, I stopped twice while showers passed, and she lifted her head to look at me with cataract-clouded eyes that, I swear, were saying she understood. Don't ever let anyone tell you dogs don't know. They do.

Unfortunately, the veterinarian's facilities didn't include a crematory. Therefore, I had to bury Misty. I laid her to rest, with her bell beside her, in the last cover we hunted. I kept her collar, of course, and it now hangs beneath one of her pictures in my den. Every now and then, usually on my way to or from new gunning grounds, I stop by that old cover—that snarled and tangled monument—just to whistle up the image of Misty and memories of the grand times and great hunting we shared.

Now you know what I mean when I say old covers remind me of abandoned cemeteries found way back in the hills.

# Wisdom of the Years

## Wisdom of the Years

"You won't believe it now," said Bill Geagan, "but you'll see the day when your desire for shooting game will diminish." I was about fifteen or so when the extremely talented outdoor writer and artist made that statement while we were sitting on the porch of the Penobscot Salmon Club. Those who remember Bill know that his love of nature and concern for Maine's fish and wildlife resources equaled or perhaps surpassed his interest in hunting and fishing.

A great friend of my grandfather's, Bill was, of course, an inspiration to me in regard to writing and art. Naturally, I took every word he spoke to be the gospel, but I must admit that I had dif-

ficulty accepting the prophecy he made that soft spring morning beside the Bangor Salmon Pool.

If Bill were alive today, though, I'd have to 'fess up and say he was right. Although my appetite for hunting hasn't diminished, I've noticed in recent years my thirst for downing game is easily quenched. But that, of course, didn't happen overnight. Well do I remember the days when I was disappointed if I didn't return home with a limit of woodcock. Worse yet were the times when I was outwitted by deer, got caught righting an overturned decoy when the morning's only flock of black ducks scaled directly over the blind, or—when trying to head off a high-geared snow-shoe hare—I arrived just in time to glimpse the hounds bounding by.

Again, it took a while, but eventually I began to wish a missed partridge good luck instead of pinpointing where it pitched down so I could whistle the dog around to find and flush it again. Likewise, I began realizing that the ducks that light outside the decoys today are the reason I'll go down to the marshes tomorrow.

Gradually, all the perspectives and proportions of the hunting scenario came into focus until the entire composition could be seen clearly. The result was a growing respect and appreciation for Mother Nature and her wonderfully wild offspring. So it was that shooting became less important to me. Sure, I still like to knock down a bird or two. That's enough to satisfy the dog and my appetite for woodcock or partridge breasts cooked in a pot of baked beans. And I still appreciate a hunting partner's, "Nice shot!" when my charge of No. 4s catches up with a wind-driven whistler. But the success of my days on the gunning grounds are no longer measured by the weight of my game bag.

Toni Hennessey —

For that reason, I have no problem with the current daily bag limits on ducks and upland game birds. If I brought home three ducks or three woodcock each time I rigged decoys or hung a bell on a bird dog, I'd have more game than my family could eat. Speaking from experience, I'll say that finding a package of duck breasts buried in the freezer is a sobering and disturbing discovery.

If you've spent a few decades behind bird dogs or occupying deer stands and duck blinds, chances are you know exactly what I'm saying. Accordingly, nowadays the memory of a flock of ringnecks roaring over the decoys means more to you than the fact that you missed them. And maybe you now smile when, leaving the woods in midmorning, you find fresh deer tracks crossing the tote road only a few feet from where you were sitting at daylight.

It's no secret that a garden must be culled as well as cultivated. So it is that controlled harvesting of game prevents overpopulation, depletion of food supplies, and death from disease and starvation. With that in mind, I can say I've done my part as a practicing conservationist, and I'm secure in the knowledge that if my self-imposed restrictions leave any slack, it will be taken up by young hunters.

In spite of all that has been written about the intricacies of shotguns and the art of wing-shooting, I realized long ago that dropping birds and ducks wasn't nearly as difficult as the "experts" make it out to be. Therefore, after fifty years of pointing and swinging shotguns at feathered game, the shooting aspect of hunting has become somewhat mechanical and insignificant.

Still important to my well-being, however, are the grand hunting traditions that I anticipate with the arrival of autumn. I enjoy guns that are getting gray, camps that are older than I am, and hunting partners who appreciate puppies full of promise but never forget the names of old dogs

whose promises were kept. I look forward to October's frost-spangled mornings and golden afternoons, a skiff of tracking snow in November, and dawn winds that shake rafts of ducks off sheets of open water in December.

Simply put, I still love hunting. But I find that nowadays my desire to kill game is diminishing. I should have known better than to doubt Bill Geagan.